Wonderfully

Loving and Teaching in a Different Light

Naima Smith Moore

Naima Smith Moore

Copyright © 2018 Naima Smith Moore

www.moorelove4yoursoul.com

All rights reserved.

ISBN: 1720999600
ISBN-13: 978-1720999607

DEDICATION

This book is dedicated to my Son, Tyler Moore as a legacy of LOVE. Mommy loves you to the moon and back. You were chosen from the womb to be different. Thank you for choosing me to be your mother and showing me how to love unconditionally. You have shown me how to be vulnerable, patient, loving, kind, sensitive, courageous, resilient, comical, generous, and creative all at the same time. I will always love you MOORE and be your number one advocate. Keep defying all odds while rocking an extra chromosome, because "Your Name is VICTORY!"

Naima Smith Moore

CONTENTS

	Acknowledgments	5
1	Childhood Memories	12
2	The Announcement	38
3	Against All Odds	55
4	A Mother's Love	72
5	His Promise Will Never Fail	85
6	His Name is Victory	95
7	Perfect Love Through Imperfection	105
8	Parent Resources	114
9	Teachers, Family, and Friends Resources	132

ACKNOWLEDGMENTS

To my Heavenly Father who has given me the strength to live, move, and have my being. For without you, I am nothing. With you, I can do all things through Christ who strengthens me. God you have stretched me, postured me, positioned me, purposed me, and given me a vision. Thank you for choosing me to carry forth the message. I honor, worship, and bless your holy name. For the Joy of the Lord is MY STRENGTH! Thank you for the anointing that dwells within me.

To my Husband: Steven Moore, thank you for loving me while being imperfectly perfect. You are the head of our family and know that I am covering us in prayer. Find your purpose, find your strength, and you will love. Always remember that words create, words construct, and words collide. Thank you for being the best dad to Tyler. We love you, but God loves you more.

To my Parents: Wayne Smith and Verrella Green, thank you for giving me life. Without you, there would be no me. Thank you for loving me and loving Tyler more. You are the best grandparents a daughter can ask for. Tyler truly loves his "Pop-Pop and Grandma V". Neither of you ever hid the truth from me and I love you for always being open and honest with me. I love you for allowing me to be an adult while still loving me unconditionally as your only child.

To my Grandma: Marjorie Morgan, I love you to no end. Without your standing in the gap, I do not know where I would be. The pages of this book may have read differently or possibly could have never been written if it weren't for you. Thank you for your unselfish love for me. You didn't have to do it, but you did, and I am forever grateful. I pray for you daily, and I hope I have made you proud.

To my Sister: Trina Diamond, I love you like the air I breathe. You are like my sister/daughter. I am so proud of the woman you have become. I love you, Melquawn and Sanna, to the moon and back. I pray daily that you find the peace, love, and joy to love life to the fullest without any worries or concerns. You know, I got you, ALWAYS, Trina-Poo.

To my Cousin/Sister: Reba Jewel, you know we go back to similac and cloth diapers, est. 1972. I love you like my sister. There is not a week that goes by that we do not speak. You are my prayer partner, my confidant, my bestie, my cousin, and my sister all rolled up into one. You are Aunt Re Lucas and Tyler loves you sometimes more than he does me. Thank you for always listening and helping to push me to greatness.

To my Spiritual Mother: Rev. Mary E. Higgs, I love, honor, and celebrate you. Thank you for pouring into my life both spiritually and naturally. Our talks and prayers make a difference, and I thank you for loving little ole me.

To my Spiritual Leaders: Rev. Lester Cousin, Rev. Erwin L. Trollinger, Rev. William C. Walker and Dr. Jonathan Shaw, I honor and celebrate you. Thank you for stretching and encouraging me while obeying the voice of God. Thank you for ministering to my life, and covering me in ministry and prayer. I am thankful to have so much spiritual guidance and grateful for your wisdom.

To my Calvary Baptist Church Family and Youth Ministry: Thank you for allowing me to serve you as I live by the motto, "To whom much is given, much is required". I love you all and get ready for the overflow...SHIFT! To God be All the Glory for the things HE is doing and continues to do.

To my Sisters: April, Tara, Shana, Claudine, KaToya, Tene, Marie, Sheila, Tameika, Battleground 914 Prayer Warriors, RAM Girls, Pastor Shauntae Smith, Min. Amy Ashley-Moore, Min. Shaunda Sutton and Min. Martina Van Norden, thank you for being an important part of my life, good, bad and pretty. Thank you for praying through and with me. I love you all. Each of you has made a unique impact, and I am grateful that we have crossed paths and remain faithful to our bond of friendship.

To my extended family: brothers, sisters, aunts, uncles, cousins, and friends, God's children, I love you all, and thank you for being a part of my life. Each one of you has made an impact on my life and I am grateful for our connection.

To my Alpha Kappa Alpha Sorority Sisters, PASHAT Family, IYM Cohort H and Work Family: Thank you for all your love and support. Each relationship means so much to me. I know I have gleaned something valuable from each of you throughout our journeys together. Keep making a difference in the lives of children. It Matters!

To Elizabeth Tabone: Thank you for seeing the vision and capturing it on canvas. Your work of art is ministry beyond the cover.

It was part of God's plan, purpose, and promise. The colors, the butterfly, the scene, and the song were all parts of the healing journey for both you and me. Continue to do what you do best, all in the name of Love.

To Fatima: Thank you for coaching and editing my first book. This was an important healing process and has been a journey of love. You have stretched me to think beyond the pages, face some difficult conversations, and produce the best of me. I am forever grateful for you, your words of encouragement, and commitment to this project.

NOTE FROM THE AUTHOR

Dear Reader,

Thank you for reading my first book. This project has been an emotional labor of love. In this book, you will read some private and detailed parts of my life that I have not shared with most. Some parts I have never expressed publicly to others, but have been a part of my personal prayers and thoughts. For those of you that know me, you know this book has been a stretch, a risk, and something way outside my comfort zone, for I am an extremely private person. This project exposes my innermost secrets and confidential thoughts to the world.

In this exposure, I hope it will liberate someone as it did for me. No longer am I a prisoner of my own truth. No longer will I hide behind others' insecurities for the sake of their feelings and my destiny. God proposed me and placed me on this earth to leave a legacy and make a difference. The fear of what others think of me will no longer have me bound. I can and will control the narration of my story and my life. This book project has truly been an expression of "Freedom" with no more mask. I did the heavy lifting so that you, reader, can see the fruits of my labor. I hope you enjoy my journey as much as I enjoyed writing about it. We are reminded daily, when we open our eyes, that we are all "Wonderfully Made, while Teaching and Loving in a Different Light!"

Love Always,

Naima

What do you do when you feel like you are doing all the right things, but you always feel different? What do you do when you are trying to do what is right, but not getting any results? There were many times when I have felt like I didn't quite fit and other times when I have felt isolated in a room full of people. Can you see me? Do you hear me? Have you looked into my eyes? Do you see my natural face? Can you see past the mask? These are questions I pondered for many years until the morning mass and my spirit were heavily anointed in a single church service in 2003.

In the back of the sanctuary, my spiritual mother, Rev. Mary E. Higgs, spoke life into her sermon, something I had always seen as different and weird. She confirmed what God had told me in a dream. She said, "You are called to preach His Gospel." Once I accepted the calling, she affirmed, I would feel so much better. She helped me understand God's intention for my life and the purpose I had in this world. I finally had an answer to my uniqueness and, finally, I felt free.

God set me apart for a reason and a purpose. His hand have always been on me, but something was holding me back. My light was not shining to its fullest potential. I was isolated and broken on the inside, worshipping with no light, praising with no light. I was looking for ways to remove God's hand, but He spoke clearly and said, "You wear a mask for the world, but I are see you in a different light."

1 CHILDHOOD MEMORIES

PROVERBS 22:6 KJV

"Train up a child in the way he should go: and when he is old, he will not depart from it."

My light has been shining at a dim wattage for as long as I can remember. I was the only child for ten years and always felt different. During my elementary school years, I was teased, bullied, and picked on. I remember that one year as if it were yesterday. Struggling with weight, I was the chubby, chocolate girl with long hair and fat cheeks. Every day, walking home from school through the park, the kids would follow me and pull my hair, ripping the hair bows out of my ponytails. Many days, I tried a different route, but they managed to find me. Whenever I strayed they ripped my clothes and coat too. Each week was something different. I had to save my allowance just to give them money for snacks afterschool. It was two of them against one of me, my friends disappearing as soon as they came around. I always questioned, why did they pick on me? Was I too nice? Did I dress too properly? Did I look like a pushover? Why me? Why not my other friends?

My mother began to question why my hair was always so messed up and barrettes were missing. She then gave a stern warning that if I came home another day with my clothes and coat torn, I was going to "get it!" It was that last statement that pushed me to stand up for myself. I was more afraid of my mother than those two bullies. I laugh about it now.

By nature, I am not a physical person nor do I like confrontation, but when backed against the wall, there is only so much a person can take. On that fall afternoon, walking through Trevor Park, they began their normal taunting, pushing, hitting, and teasing. I warned them, trying to be polite, but they only laughed. Then, I remembered what my mother told me. I grabbed the smaller of the two girls and went to work. Needless to say, when the nearby adult pulled me off of her, the other children who had been watching, including her friend, were standing with their hands over their mouths, pointing and snickering at the other girl.

Although I felt victorious, I did not like the fact that there I could have done some serious damage to another human being with my own hands out of anger. When I was banging the girls head on the concrete, I wanted to stop, but I was so angry from all the times she picked on me. I could not bring myself to stop. I could hear the other kids shouting, "Stop, Nikki. You are going to hurt her." But, in that moment, I could not. I was only capable of thinking about the times when I asked them to stop picking on me and they would not. There was never a single person around to convince them to stop, force them to.

Now, the irony to this story is, I never told my mother what was happening all along. So, when I walked in the house after school and the fight, my mom greeted me at the door with a voice of chastisement. Can you believe the two young ladies went home to their parents and said I physically assaulted one of them, conveniently leaving out our history? Initially, I was punished for beating up the smaller girl. When my mom heard my side of the story and all the history behind my anger, however, we had a meeting with their mothers. Fortunately, my story resulted in positive outcomes. The first, I stood up for myself. Second, my mom advocated for me.

That being said, how many of our children are suffering in silence because they are different and afraid to stand up for themselves or tell an adult? I made a promise at that point in my life that if I ever became a parent, I would look for subliminal warnings and signs, probe for questions and do unannounced visits to schools.

During my tween and teenage years, many changes took place. Our family dynamic changed from my being an only child to two brown girls being reared by a single mom. In the early 1980's, not only did the family structure change, but the community did also. Drugs hit the African American low-income community hard, particularly crack-cocaine. What was once a family oriented, kid friendly neighborhood had turned into what looked like a scene from a war-zone. The neighborhood went from having an open campus feel to having security, doors with buzzers, barbed wire fences, surveillance cameras, and police that patrolled regularly. Before, we would occasionally worry about broken glass on the playground, but soon we were finding used needles and crack valves with different color tops everywhere on a regular basis. We began to hear gun shots frequently, always followed by sounds of police sirens. Men and women we once looked up to looked like zombies walking on the street. They begged for money and sometimes asked to perform sexual tricks in return for drugs or a quick hit. The community change began to filter into our home. Almost instantly, I went from being a big sister who loved to play carelessly with her little sister after school to the big sister who had to assume motherly responsibilities due to an absent mom.

After years of wishing for a sister, I quickly resented the seizure of my childhood without a choice. I had the responsibility of picking up my sister, a toddler at the time, from the babysitter, and caring for her until my mom came home from work. There were days of disappearance. There was no food, no direction. I had to try to figure out how to eat and get clean clothes. Sometimes, I had to find a way out of the locked house, with a key that only my mother possessed. There were many questions as to why my mom did what she did. Was it to keep us safe and secure inside? Or, perhaps, was it to keep the bad people out? That, I always wondered.

Eventually, we ended up living with the babysitter. At that time, my mom was absent from our lives, and I was left with many questions and concerns. I wondered where she was. Was she coming back? And why, did she leave us? She was gone, and that made me even more different. There were days when I just wanted to be a kid. I wanted to play and have a mother to hold me, hug me, take me out to dinner, get my hair done, or curl up with to a book or a good television show.

But, I didn't have that, and, naturally, rebellion set in. It began to manifest in staying out late, stealing, and taking an interest in boys who validated my insecurities and filled the void of what I thought was love. After excessively missing school, rapidly declining grades, and a growing numbness for life, it was decided that I would go live with my maternal grandmother. For a short time, she provided me with a sense of stability, and a glimpse of light on cloudy days.

However, that feeling of isolation and loneliness soon returned because my sister was no longer with me. With two different fathers, she went to live with her dad in Brooklyn, NY while I went to our grandmothers' home in White Plains, NY. My grandmother was willing to take one of us, but she could not take on the responsibility of two children especially a toddler who was neither self-sufficient nor in school.

The transition was messy and confusing. It was filled with court sessions, arguments, and ultimately a three year period during which I did not see my sister. The newness of living with my grandmother was both happy and sad. There were times I wanted to be alone, so I retreated to my room. There were also times when I just wanted to have my mother love on me. These were more common as I watched some of my friends bond with their mothers. I longed for womanly conversations about puberty. All I wanted was to say, "I love you mom!" I made up my mind and decided if I ever got the opportunity to become a mother, I would love my child by being the best mom I could be, and make sure I did everything to ensure that I kept our family together.

During this transition, routines and stability became important to me. My grandmother did everything she could to comply. Every day after work, she would send me to the corner store for a soda and to play her lottery numbers. This became comforting to me. The ability to go to the store without embarrassment because we did not have the money to purchase what was on the list and return home without fear of abandonment was important to me.

But, there were some growing pains while I adjusted to life with my grandmother. I had to remember that she was the adult and I was the child. Having to make adult decisions on my own for such a long period of time, one could only imagine that was not an easy habit to break. I also had to break the habit of stealing money because often times I knew no other way to survive the day.

In addition, I had to learn new roles in my living arrangement. My grandmother provided a home that was loving, while exhibiting what it meant to be a responsible adult. She allowed me to watch her doing grown up things such as cooking, cleaning, and disciplining. She provided the basic necessities of life and monitored my actions. Coming from a place that lacked discipline, moving into a home that was very regulated was, at most times, uncomfortable on the surface, but also, on occasion, warming to the heart and soul. It eased my anxiety and worries about day-to-day survival.

But, I still had habits that needed adjusting. My grandmother was displeased with my behavior, which was causing a strain on our relationship. Eventually, she had to sit me down in the presence of my father to lay down the ground rules, which I had to obey if I wished to continue living there. These changes were to be made in school, at home, and in my overall demeanor.

I had no other options; I was at the end of my choices. My mother was gone. And my father was not an option. Although present in my life, my dad was often absent in his physical contact with me. He had started another family, and it was clear that I was not openly welcomed by his new wife. Once again, a feeling of abandonment and poor representation of what a male should be to a woman lead me to making poor choices in male companionship.

However, that was not the only motivation. I also didn't want to disappoint my grandmother. So, I decided to pick a different group of peers to call my friends. I found one friend who displayed the qualities that I wanted to emulate: high standards, excellence, honor roll, and no drama. Peer pressure was not easy to resist, but I hated the ten week punishments, daily quizzes, chores, and lists of things I could not do even more.

During this time, the true reset button was pressed. Through my pain, a purpose was birthed, and a determination was ignited. My goal was to successfully complete middle and high school. I needed to work hard and make connections, so college could become possible. However, I couldn't read very well, unlike math which I could do in my sleep. I didn't read with fluency or comprehension. I struggled with word pronunciation, vocabulary, and reading comprehension and speed. Most times, I had to read a passage several times to understand what was happening. I would fumble over words, and nothing was ever of interest to me because of that. I was never able to relate the literature I was reading to what was happening in my life, which made the task daunting and laborious. As a result, standardized tests that required large amounts of reading kept the odds stacked against me. But, I knew I couldn't let it hold me back. The thought of not attending college was not an option. It was my only way out of the cycle of mediocrity. So, I knew I had to work harder than my peers, getting extra help when needed. All I needed to succeed was hope.

During high school, I met the person who would become my life's mentor, Sandra E. Burno-DeBerry. She was my computer, typing, and business teacher. She fed me the idea and possibility of a life of hope. In addition to her, was my youth group leader, Heather Miller. Her passion and love for us was so obvious, so palpable that she sparked a light in me, too. She inspired the "by any means necessary" spirit. The love they exuded was infectious. They exposed me to life beyond the school building by getting me involved in community groups and volunteering. They saw and drew out leadership qualities inside me that I could not find within myself.

I remember the first time I was invited to attend a Martin Luther King Jr. club meeting at the Greenburgh Community Center. This was an exciting and pivotal point in shaping my future. Every Monday evening, we met and discussed current events in our country, how things impacted our community, volunteering opportunities, planning for college tours, and preparing for academic success. On Saturdays, we visited local New York colleges. On one particular trip, we attended a meeting with a group of executives from Cigna Corporation that agreed to sponsor us on an all-expense paid trip to Atlanta, Georgia to tour a college tour and Martin Luther King, Jr.'s birth house, adult home, church, and grave site. This was a time in my life filled with milestones. It was my first time on an airplane, my first time entering the grounds of a historically black university campus, and my first time going into a bookstore, picking up the book, "I Know Why the Caged Bird Sings" by Maya Angelou, the first piece of literature I had an immediate connection to. It was the first time I read a book for pleasure, from beginning to end, by someone who looked like me. That initiated my thirst for African American literature from African American.

Although, late in my high school years, my desire for and focus on a new genre of writing helped me craft a decent college essay and receive SAT scores that got me into North Carolina Central University. While on a college tour there, they treated me like a family member which was the deciding factor for my school decision.

During my freshman year in college, my poor reading skills were still quite apparent. I had to take remedial English and Math classes because I did not score well on the basic college exams for those subjects. This did not stop me from excelling, however. I began to set goals each semester regarding my grades, and planned to graduate within four years.

I went to NCCU all the way from New York, not knowing how I was going to pay for college. As the first in my family to attend college, I had no blueprint or pattern to follow. When we arrived in Durham, NC I had not even completed the financial aid packet. I did not know which questions to ask or not to ask. In fact, I only sent in the deposit for the room and nothing else. It was by the grace of God that when we stood on that long line on that hot August day in 1990 that the woman in the financial aid office was a Christ follower who believed in me. At first, my grandmother had to fill out paperwork and take out a parent loan, but by September of 1990, my dad was able to cover the expenses. Can you say that we serve a God who is a provider? He is the Way, He is the Truth, and He is the Light!

From that day in 1990 until May of 1994, I went to the Bursar's office to pay a small bill, leaving the majority of the costs covered simply from building relationships, receiving scholarships, and by the grace of God. Preparation for the future was being provided, yet I had no idea. Throughout the process of obtaining an advances degree in business finance, the ministry of working with children pulled at my heart strings. So, during my spare time, I volunteered at the local community center as a youth advisor where I met weekly with students in order to allow them to express their views about things happening in their world, how they wanted to give back to the greater community, and how they wanted to engage their peers. We had guest speakers that spoke with students regarding schooling, financial management, resume/job building, and community service. While working with the Thomas H. Slater Center INVEST Youth Council, I learned to appreciate and value the truth of young people. I was able to see them for who they were, listen to their dreams and aspirations, and speak life into those same things. It was during this time that I knew I had a different assignment and calling in my career path. God had positioned His light differently on my life. I did not understand while I was going through each obstacle, but now I do. My light had to be different because my position was different, so I could tell my story to deliver someone else out of tribulation.

My life stands as a tale to let you know that God can do things exceedingly and abundantly above all you could ask or think.

As I continued in the business field through banking and finance, the routine of work was there, but the joy, love, and immediate satisfaction were not. What I talked about most was what I did for children. What lit up my face and my heart was what I could do to put a smile on a child's face. Others were able to see and feel the joy of my soul when I spoke about the experiences I had with children helping to shape their lives, minds, and goals for the future. The question was often asked, why don't you pursue a career in the field of education? The thought crossed my mind often, but I felt if I followed my dreams I would have wasted a large portion of my time, education, money, and familial sacrifices to start all over again on a different career path that was not in the scope of my current field of study.

The calling and tugging of my spirit continued for almost ten years. Within this timeframe I climbed the corporate ladder from banking to finance to completing my Series 6 and 63 to completing a Master's in Business Administration in Finance and Human Resource Management. I pondered the questions, how can I leave all this hard work behind? How can I waist time and money already invested? However, I was not happy or fulfilled in what I was doing. I was always told I completed my job well, but the immediate gratification and appreciation was never present. Most times it felt like it was a thankless job, especially when dealing with an individual's money.

The more I worked with children, teenagers, and families, the more I felt a sense of immediate gratification whether I helped a student solve a problem, affirmed a family, or was just there to support a student at in important event. Students gave hugs, laughs, and tears, in pain, joy, hope, and accomplishment. Why not become a teacher? That question lingered for years.

On the morning of September 11th, 2001, I was driving to work. All the radio stations were being interrupted with breaking news followed by silence. I remember going into work and immediately entering one of the only conference rooms that housed a television with cable reception. All the Vice Presidents and Directors gathered in the room and we all watched one tower burn, a plane fly into the second tower, both buildings burn, and reporters trying to report the tragedy. Then came the collapse. Debris was everywhere. People were screaming. Then the television went blank. It was a day the world stood still. Many people lost their lives, and for me, it was a reality check, a moment to decide if this career ws really what I wanted, what I needed or if there was a higher calling and purpose in my life.

A flood of emotions flashed before me on that day. My dad was in the city, and I had other family members and close friends who worked in the immediate area. As a company and team, we prayed, cried, tried expressing what we felt, and reached out to loved ones. Then, the building went into emergency response mode during which everyone's true nature came out. The children in my youth group became a concern immediately. It was important for me to try to reach out to them, but the phone lines and e-mails were all jammed. It became nearly impossible to get through. Anxiety levels in the office were heightened, but my focus was that the children in the youth group had someone to talk, hug, encourage them, and to help them sort out their feelings and concerns. This was the foundation of my passion of working with children, loving children and knowing that I could change the lives of and advocate for children and families as well who could not do the same for themselves.

Years later, in July of 2003, I was scheduled to go on an all-inclusive Caribbean vacation with my friends. A much needed vacation at that. Unbeknownst to me, my vacation was scheduled on the half year reporting deadline, which was crucial for budget season and forecasting for the last half of the year. There were two areas that did not have their numbers ready. It was a Friday, and my plane was departing the next afternoon. At 3:05 pm, my manager came over to my desk with information to let me know that the two area managers needed until Monday to complete their parts. Therefore, I would be unable to leave for vacation until at least Wednesday. This was the breaking point that was pivotal in my move from a corporate career to formally applying to become an educator. At that moment, I had to weigh the importance of happiness over money, peace of mind over ambiguity. I had to live and step out on Hebrews 11: 1, "Now, faith is the substance of things hoped for, the evidence of things not seen." It was scary. I was being stretched, not sure how bills would get paid because I was taking a significant pay cut.

However, I prayed to God and asked Him to open all doors, provide, and supply all my needs if this were, in fact, His will. I began to research how I could use my business background to obtain a teaching certification and career. My goal was to find out what I needed from the New York State Education Department to become a business education teacher. In the meantime, I had to step out on faith and apply for a job.

In August, 2003, I went to a job fair, completed the writing sample, interviewed on the spot, and was offered to come back in for a second interview. Things happened so fast. By the second week that month, I was given an offer to become a business teacher. Now, look at God. He will provide. When I looked at the letter, I almost fell out of my seat because it was almost half of my current salary. I had to pray hard, negotiate a little more, but not much could be done. I had to really budget and believe that God would supply all of my needs. For Mark 11: 24 says, "Therefore I say unto you, what things so ever ye desire, when ye pray, believe that ye receive them, and ye shall have them."

So, I went into my director's office and gave in my resignation letter. I shared with him my new career aspirations and goals. He laughed at first because he thought I was playing, but when he realized I was serious, provided encouraging words, leaving an open offer of return if I changed my mind. The foundation of planting seeds on good, fertile ground had begun.

As I wrote this book, it occurred to me that God allowed me to go back to my childhood city where I went to elementary school, the foundation of my education, to also be the foundation of my career. He gave me the ability to relate to our children in disadvantaged situations, to allow them to see me and have hope. He helped me show them that although the poor circumstances may be there, it doesn't have to define them or mark the ends of their journeys. The foundation was awesome, the experience was awesome, and the children were awesome. Despite the area, the students produced the best for me. They had creative minds and willing spirits filled with love. The students enjoyed coming to class, and I enjoyed having them. The transition from corporation to education was seamless. It felt natural, as if it were supposed to be.

Working With Children Who Are Different

Although I taught elective classes, I was blessed to tailor the same curriculum to students who learned differently. Early in my career, I discovered there was a special place in my heart for students who presented and thought differently. These young people gravitated towards me, many times just to get a hug. My colleagues would caution me about giving hugs to a child. One day I spoke up and said, "I'm not worried, because it is all done in love. God's got my back, and this may be the only hug and love our children receive today." From that point on, I knew I had made the right decision. All that I lost financially would be regained through the seeds that had been planted. Seeds of LOVE.

My first teaching assignment was in Yonkers Public Schools at Commerce Middle School. It served as a training ground for what was to come. In addition, it brought me back to the beginning of my life, my roots, and my educational experience. It brought me back to a place where the wounds of the hurt, abandonment, promiscuity, molestation, abuse, hunger, separation, poverty, and addiction all took place. I had to come back to the beginning, to connect, build relationships, and dig up what was suppressed in order to move forward and be successful. The children that sat before me every day for the first year acted as daily reminders of who I was, where I had come from, and the miracles that God had placed in my life. I had to go back to the beginning so I did not allow myself to stay or remain in the spirit of my circumstance. It was only God who allowed me to become transparent, real, and compassionate. It was only God who helped me tell my story to the one hundred fifty sixth grader students, staff, and administrators. I wanted to spark a spirit of hope, connect with a group of students who learned differently, and allow them to feel like a part of the school community rather than outcasts.

Throughout that year, I was able to teach business concepts to middle school students in both a traditional and an untraditional way. We ventured through the curriculum by using a book study. We read about entrepreneurial activities, marketing, financing activities, advertisement, and accounting. We created a school wide store during the lunch period which sold unique snacks and school supplies. Students understood and applied the concepts of supply and demand. Lastly, we created advertisements and marketing campaigns based on a theme from the book, *The Toothpaste Millionaire* by Jean Merrill.

Students were able to peer evaluate, record and review their peers work, and create a product for sale.

In April, 2004, I received a pink slip. A pink slip was put in my mailbox at work with a statement that explained my position was being eliminated and I would be out of a job. Immediately, I felt anxious and feared the unknown, as I had been employed since the age of fifteen. This was a new feeling and I did not like it because I was not in control of the outcome. The only option I had was to lean and depend on God. I believed and had faith that God did not allow me to go through this entire process and career change, fall in love with children, and get instant gratification from children and parents, just to leave me to figure it all out on my own. There had to be something greater in store for me, something bigger, beyond my own frame of thought, dreams, and imagination.

Just as I began to pray and truly give all my burdens to the Lord, that glimpse of light opened. An opening for a high school business position became available at my high school alma mater. When one talks about something coming full circle, this is truly an example of a full circle experience. To begin working where one's educational experiences first started and then end up where God had destined one to live greater and with a purpose was beyond words. This was an opportunity to impact lives and give back to the same community that spoke life into the shell of a brown girl. A brown girl who was riddled with trauma, pain, hurt, abandonment, and no blueprint to follow. A brown girl who was the first in her family to break the cycle and attend a four year institution of higher education. A brown girl who was predestined to create her own pattern to follow and know that it was by the grace of God she made it this far. This was an opportunity to work with some of the very same people who changed my life and have a major impact on the future generations of graduates at White Plains High School. To a teacher in the very same halls that I spent my adolescent years in was a dream come true.

As I sat in the Student Government Office awaiting my interview, the energy, the hustle and bustle of high school children and adults, was exciting and felt right. The joy in my spirit and soul exploded out my pores and said so clearly that this was home. The warmth of greetings and the exchange of smiles made the divine connection ever so real and in sync. Upon leaving the interview, my level of confidence and the dialogue that had taken place reassured me that, *this is so.* The magic truly displayed itself when I had an opportunity to demonstrate my skills in front of a class of students that I did not know. It all came down to relationship building and understanding how to connect to our children regardless of their race, religion or ethnic backgrounds. The common denomination that connects us all is LOVE.

During the next seven years, I met the love of my life, got married, and dedicated my life to ensuring that the same love, resources, and opportunities that were afforded to me were now returned even more to my students. To whom much is given, much is required. That is the motto I live by. I believe that we have a responsibility to teach and reach our younger generations, and to do so in love. We must set a standard and be the role model they can refer to at all times. In my time as a high school teacher, I stayed late, participated as an extracurricular advisor to several clubs in and out of school, opened my home to feed our children, and became the voice of reason who listened when it was needed most. Due to my classroom location, I had the ability to interact with all students of many different abilities. The highlight of my day was when I stood at my door in the hall during the change of periods, and two students with Trisomy 21 (Down Syndrome) would run to me, give me a hug, say hello, and call me mom. They were my pride and joy, while others saw them in a different light.

God always works perfectly. All things happen in His timing. God answered my secret prayers of having my mom recover. He placed me in a school that allowed me to work with amazing young people. Little did I know he was preparing me for everything else that was to come.

Chapter 1 Reflection (Use the space below to jot down your thoughts)

1. Think about a time during your childhood when you faced a challenge, how did you get through? Who was helpful in getting you through those challenging times?

2. What do you think are some steps an adult can take to help a child who may be experiencing some challenges at school or at home?

3. Rehearse with a partner how you would express your "truth". How do you know when to listen to that inner voice? What steps do you take?

2 THE ANNOUNCEMENT

JEREMIAH 1:5

"Before I formed thee in the belly I knew thee; and before thou camest forth out of the womb I sanctified thee, and I ordained thee a prophet unto the nations."

In May 2008, I went on a girl's trip to Chicago to see my bestie who was on a work assignment. We were excited to see her and experience all the Windy City had to offer. Our flight arrived to Chi-town late and we were all very hungry. Among my friends, we all know that I absolutely love dessert, especially warm brownies with vanilla bean ice cream, and a drizzle of hot caramel. I love it so much so, that I will forgo food, a regular meal, and have dessert first. When we finally arrived at the apartment from the airport, my girlfriend had dinner prepared. She cooked baked ziti, garlic bread, tossed salad, and, of course, since she knows me so well, she prepared my favorite dessert, warm brownies with ice cream. For some reason, I passed on having dessert first and went for the food. Everyone looked at me strangely. But, I ignored their looks and went to work on the ziti, which was top notch. It was banging. It was as if my Nana herself had stepped into that Chicago kitchen, prepared the food, and flown back to New York all in a blink of an eye. I inhaled that food like a vacuum cleaner. My friends again looked at me strangely. For one, I ate my food really quickly, which was very unusual since I'm always the last one to finish. Second, I ate a second and third plate of ziti, something I never do because I always save room for dessert. Lastly, I declined having dessert that evening.

One of my friends flat out asked me, "are you okay, and are you pregnant?"

I said, "Oh, no, my cycle is actually due tomorrow. I'm good."

With a side eye, she said, "okay, let me know if we need to go get a pregnancy test."

"Oh, girl, No! We are good!" I said. I took a shower and immediately went to bed, no second thoughts.

The next morning, I was famished as if I had nothing to eat the night before. We grabbed granola bars, fruit, and some snacks to go as we had a tight itinerary to follow for the day. While in the car, I noticed my sense of smell was heightened. I could smell every little thing, even those silent but violent smells that slipped out from one of my friends before the masses could smell it. My one friend that did not have a healthy relationship with dairy could not understand how I was the only one that could smell it before everyone else. To be honest, so was I.

While on our walking tour in Chicago, toward HARPO studios and the Navy Pier, I began to feel funny, almost light headed. It felt as if I was going to faint. I needed something in my body to eat or drink or maybe just sit down. If not, it was not going to be a favorable sight. At that very moment, I knew something was not right. The chemical balance in my body was off. I was getting hot and cold. I was thirsty, and I felt butterflies in my stomach. I ate some peanuts hoping to settle my stomach, but that was not enough. I began to get irritable. All these behaviors were not normal for me. The feelings would come and go throughout the weekend, and I never saw my menstrual cycle while on the trip. But, I did not mention it to any of my friends because I wanted my husband to be the first to know if we were pregnant.

As soon as I got home, I made sure my first priority was to go to the drug store for an over-the-counter pregnancy test. I went home, followed the directions on the box, waited for the results, and then waited patiently for my husband to come home from work to tell him the news. I was overjoyed, anxious, and nervous all at the same time. I had waited to share that particular moment with my husband for what seemed like forever. This was the first time it felt right, like it was a blessing not a generational curse or a cycle of poor choices and bad behaviors. This was the first time the response was not going to be "so, what are you going to do?" This was the first time I did not feel like I was in a low place. I was happy, in love, accepted, and wanted. I was going to have a family and we were all going to have the same last name.

On June 25th, 2008, I went for my first prenatal sonogram. This was the ultimate thirty sixth birthday gift for me. We sat in the room, and on the screen I viewed my womb and the pea sized element of life in black and white form. The heartbeat penetrated through the speakers like the beat of a drum to let us know there was life. That life belonged to two people who created it out of love. Just when we thought there may be a possibility of never conceiving, when family members planted a seed of doubt by questioning age, when we were almost ready to throw in the towel, God stepped in. He always manages to shine a different light on a situation when it is least expected.

My announcement left me feeling elated, overjoyed, excited, and super awesome. I didn't experience morning sickness or stress. I made sure to drink plenty of fluids and got lots of rest. I know most women experience weird cravings, but I didn't. And as much as I love sweets, I did not have a desire for anything sweet. No desserts! Having a life growing inside of you is the weirdest feeling ever, but at the same time, awesomeness to the highest power. All I wanted was apples, meat, and guacamole. I was losing weight, and gaining muscle and good fat. During my pregnancy I realized how the body is miraculous and the mind an amazing muscle. In my first trimester, I developed post nasal drip that made me cough all day and night. However, the very first day of my second trimester, it disappeared. My connection to and love for the baby was immediate. I began reading and talking to the baby, letting the baby know that he/she was loved. Then, the journaling process began.

In August 2008, while preparing to go on my annual vacation south, I was driving to my sorority sister's house to finish up some last minute financial business. On my way to her home, I received a phone call from the obstetrician/gynecologist.

The call went like this, "Naima, is this Naima Moore?"

"Yes, this is she," I said.

"Hello, this is your doctor. We received the results back from your labs."

"Okay, let me pull over, so I can write if I need to. Please give me a second to do so," I requested, and then pulled over into the parking lot of Mighty Joe Young's Steakhouse.

"Naima."

"Yes, I'm ready. Go ahead," I said, unprepared for what I was going to hear.

"I'm sorry to inform you that your results have come back, and your unborn child will be born with Down syndrome. We need you to..."

At that point she was talking, and it felt like my whole world had caved on top of the car with no way out. I was overtaken with emotions, with a million questions at once, with guilt, with fear, with pain. That joy that I had felt at the beginning disappeared. It felt as though someone sucked the life out of me in one blow.

The next thing I heard her say was, "Naima are you there? I am going to need you to make an appointment with the perinatologist, a genetics specialist, and then come in to see me to let me know what your final decision will be."

I was numb, paralyzed and stuck all at the same time.

"Naima are you there…"

As the tears began to run down this brown girls face, I began to feel a pain, unbearable pain, pain in my soul, as I sat in my car and had to endure this news all by myself. It hurt to my core to the point where I tried to speak but nothing would come out of my mouth. It was pain that pierced my heart and finally I let out a screeching sound of, "NO, WHY ME LORD, WHY ME! What did I do to deserve this?"

The doctor sat in silence and then said, "I'm sorry Naima, once you make a decision, please call us and let us know."

I took down the information and hung up. I mustered up enough strength and called my sorority sister to tell her I would have to come by another day due to an emergency. Immediately afterwards, I called my husband, and, through my hysterical crying, he managed to calm me down so he could understand what I was trying to say. The words that mattered the most that day were said by my husband, "God blessed us with a child, and, no matter the disability, we are still going to love that child with every fiber of our beings."

I thank God every day for the blessing of Tyler Steven Moore because he shows me how to love in a different light. Tyler has shown me what unconditional love truly means. He has shown me that love is patient, kind, gentle, passionate, trusting, hopeful, pure, slow to anger and easy to forgive, understanding, willing to compromise, not puffed up, and it never fails. He has shown me that no matter what the circumstance God's answer is always yes and amen. He has shown me that no matter what God is always in control of the situation. He has shown me that no matter what God will lead and guide so long as we sit still long enough to communicate, listen, and follow. He has shown me that no matter what, GOD IS! God is not a punishing God. He is a God of blessings. Many times, we allow ourselves to compare our children and lives to others. We allow ourselves to set a standard of what is right and what is wrong by what others are doing or what others have. As a result, we formulate a thought process that is as follows: if we don't live up to the standards of the world, we have failed, or God is not pleased at what we are doing, so this is our payback.

Often times, as parents of children with different abilities, we see our children as God's punishment to something we have done in the past. Our God is not a punishing God. He is a God of blessings. For the Bible says, "Be not conformed to this world, but be ye transformed, by the renewing of your mind." Our minds have to be renewed and reminded that our God makes no mistakes. Tyler chose me as his mother. This was in God's divine plan. For God knew then, that the pages of this book were in his plans. Jeremiah 29:11 reminds us that, "For I know the plans I have for you, declares the Lord, plans to prosper you and not to harm you, plans to give you hope and a future."

Educating oneself during pregnancy is overwhelming within itself, but now we had to add an additional language with all the new acronyms of students with special needs and doctors' appointments to the To-Do list. When I went to my first perinatologist visit, it was great to see that the doctor was a professional brown man. He presented me with the options of the pregnancy and possibilities of difficulties of rearing a child with a different ability, with Down syndrome, and the spectrum of differences within the disability. I immediately explained to the doctor, to whom I belonged, and the blessing that God had given us. I immediately declared that this child would be a blessing to many and defy all odds.

The doctor smiled and said, "I must provide you with all the information, but I am elated that you are a believer."

That was all the confirmation I needed. The genetic counselor wanted to do an amniocentesis, but I refused. The chances of survival were fifty percent, so my faith went into overdrive. During this incubation period, I had double the appointments. The perinatologist's primary concerns were to measure the bone growth and heart chambers of the fetus. The doctor said from the womb Tyler would be different. His heart was strong. His bones were growing great, and he was extremely active in my womb. Despite this, I did not discuss the possibility of my child's having a different ability. I spoke life into my unborn child. I anointed my body, my womb. I prayed and declared greatness of life over my unborn child. I spoke purpose in the life of my unborn child. I believed that God would do supernatural miracles and change things around for His good. In that last month of pregnancy, we began to experience some complications. The baby's heart rate began to drop during the monitoring sessions, which indicated the baby was under duress. The ultrasound could not detect what the cause was because the baby was too big in the womb. Three times in a five week period, we had to return to the hospital for monitoring because we thought it was going to be an emergency delivery. At this point my doctor changed my mode of delivery from natural child birth to cesarean section.

On January 23rd, 2009, at 9:03 a.m., Tyler Steven Moore was born weighing seven pounds and nine ounces, eighteen inches long, delivered by C-section. Thanks be to God that we delivered by C-section because the umbilical cord was wrapped around Tyler's neck, which was the cause of his declining heart rate. Had I tried to deliver naturally, Tyler would have died during delivery. They cleaned him up, and I held him for a brief minute. Then, off to the NICU he went.

After doing a series of blood test, and looking at one of his hands, indicating an extraneous chromosome via a single crease line, it was determined that Tyler had Trisomy 21, also known as Down

Syndrome. As with any disability, there is a range in severity. Each child is different. Hence, Tyler is seen in a different light.

I went an entire day without seeing my child. I neither knew what was going on nor was anyone explaining anything to me. I couldn't move the lower half of my body because I had to wait for the anesthesia to wear off. There was one lady who introduced herself as the social worker. She kept coming in and asking when my husband was coming back. I knew something did not feel right, so I called my husband and told him to come up to the hospital immediately. When he finally arrived, the doctor and the social worker came into the room to talk to us about Tyler's diagnosis and disability. The genetic test result came back with a positive result of Trisomy 21 (Down syndrome). They went over what the results meant and what we were to expect as parents. That overwhelming feeling resurfaced from the initial announcement, similar to that of the parking lot experience at the beginning of the chapter. I felt like I was going to hyperventilate and the mere fact that they had not allowed me to see or touch my baby was all overwhelming. Here I was, strangers talking to me about options, support, numbers, filling out paperwork, and asking questions. Again, I felt numb, both figuratively and literally. I felt helpless, lost, confused, and alone. I just wanted to start all over again. I tried to remain strong. However, the emotions that were overtaking my body from the pit of my stomach up to my throat as if I was going to choke or vomit took over. When everyone left, including my husband, I cried uncontrollably. God gave me everything I asked for. I thought I did things the right way. So, why is this happening to me? Why did I feel empty, isolated, broken and with no light? Why God, Why?

I pulled myself up, and slowly, one step at a time, walked to the NICU. I needed to touch him, smell him, and see the life that grew inside of me for thirty nine weeks. I needed clarity as to why he was in the NICU. When I got there, he was being prepped for a changing. I was just on time to scrub in and change him. Well, low and behold, Tyler urinated on me. Once we cleaned up, I was able to kangaroo hold him. They took the oxygen off him, and he opened his eyes at the sound of my voice. Love in action, and he no longer needed oxygen to assist his breathing. Tyler needed to know that his mother was there to love and hold him unconditionally. It was a love like I had never encountered, pure and untainted. I felt this way about my son. Now, just imagine how God feels about us. God loves us all so much that he gave us His only son, so that we would not die or perish in our sins. If we only just believe in him and confess with our mouth that he is Lord, we will be saved.

When I returned to my hospital room, I prayed and had a little talk with God.

The conversation went like this, "God, my Father, Thank you for being the Great I am, Creator of Heaven and Earth, the One who spoke light into existence. Thank you for my blessing in the form of life through Tyler Steven Moore. To the visual eyes, he is perfect. He has all of his limbs, no more or less. His organs are functioning, and he is sustaining life on his own. So thank you, Lord, in advance, for the victory. You are awesome in all your works. Whatever may come in the future, we count it victorious right now in the name of Jesus. No weapon formed against us will prosper. You have gotten us to this point and Tyler will defeat all odds. He will be your living, walking, visual testimony of what you can do, if we only believe. It is in Jesus' name that it is done. Amen."

I prayed that prayer. I journaled it in my book and closed my eyes to rest for the evening. It was not until the next day, when I had to explain and repeat his diagnosis to others that the pain, doubt, and fear began to creep in once again. I could not talk about it without crying. My mind was not right. My mind had a different type of vocabulary than what reality had positioned me for. You see, I had planned for one thing, and, now, I had to reprogram my thinking to incorporate the reality.

My life would now consist of therapists, doctor's appointments, specialists, and juggling schedules around an already busy life. My mind was not present, and each time I had to explain his diagnosis or give a family history or another document, it was as if I were relieving the first time all over again. I thought the more I talked about it, the better it would get. However, it appeared to get worse. The more I talked about it the worse I felt. I wanted to wish his different ability away. I tried calling the support groups that the social worker gave me from the hospital, and they either did not call me back or the person on the other end sounded preoccupied with his own stuff or I didn't feel a connection. It felt useless. I felt like I was going to have to endure this alone, as if no one could relate to what I was going through. I found myself crying all the time. Each time I had to talk about Tyler and his different ability, I cried. I cried because I felt alone and none of my friends had to endure what I had to go through. There was no one I could turn to for advice. I felt isolated and alone once again, and not part of the circle of friends. I began to blame myself. I began to question if it was me because, the fact was, my husband had three children already, all free of any disabilities. I cried because I didn't know what I was going to do. I cried because I was not in control. I cried because I did not know what to expect. I cried because I knew that people would look at us differently. I cried because I felt as though no one would understand. Each time I talked about him, I truly had to renew my mind to know that Tyler was wonderfully made.

Chapter 2 Reflection (Use space below to jot down thoughts)
1. What do you do when what you have prayed for is different than what God has planned for your life?

2. Discuss the possible pros and cons of rearing a child with special needs.

3. What do you do when you need to have a "come to Jesus moment"?

3 AGAINST ALL ODDS

1 JOHN 4:4

"Ye are of God, little children, and have overcome them: because greater is he that is in you, than he that is in the world."

I prayed more. I read more. I researched more. My feeling did not get better. My health started spiraling. I started gaining weight, my blood pressure increased, and I began having issues with fibroids. I went to what comforted me the most, food, junk food at that.

Initially, I thought the announcement of having a baby would draw us closer as a family, but like with anything else, it presented challenges that were unexpected. Due to the C-section, I was limited to what I could do, and how I could move. I felt frustrated because I was used to being in control, and now I felt helpless. In addition to frustration and declining health, I had to incorporate interviewing early intervention therapists, doctors, case workers while concurrently trying to recuperate and be a wife and a mom to a newborn.

While going through the paperwork and reading what the possibilities of Tyler's future may look like, I had to find a way to clear my mind and change my mindset. I literally had to have a "come to Jesus" moment with myself. I had to search the scriptures and not allow what I was reading on the medical papers or hearing from professionals to take root in my mind and soul. For Romans 12:2 says, "and be not conformed to this world: but be ye transformed by the renewing of your mind, that ye may prove what is that good, and acceptable, and perfect, will of God." I had to be my own hype woman, convincing and encouraging myself by saying, "You got this woman. Everything is going to be okay. God is not going to leave you or forsake you. He is not going to give you more than you can bare. This is only a test." I remember one time, I was sitting on my bed trying to pump breast milk. I was encouraging myself while crying because the pump was not working right.

However, it is was easier said than done. When you are living through those moments of shame and guilt, having to explain why Tyler's breathing sounded as if it was a rattling sound in his throat, called a strider, was not easy. It was not easy when people were unkind and or lacked mindfulness in their thoughts and comments.

It really bothered me when people, faces balled up as if they were looking at a foreign object, would ask what was wrong with him. As a parent with a child with a different ability, you always find yourself on the defensive, ready to protect, and always feeling the need to explain. It is exhausting! Most people do not realize what they are doing and how difficult they are making life for a parent when they are not informed or compassionate, but are quick to make negative comments. As my son's number one advocate, I had to make sure that I was the best person I could be in order to help others understand Tyler, and how they could help him. I had to understand how I could be the best mom, educator, administrator, and advocate for Tyler.

Upon discharge from the hospital, we were told that Tyler did not pass the hearing test and that he may be deaf. We were told he needed to see an audiologist to have his hearing checked again for a second opinion. At that moment, I felt as though my faith was being tested and I had no other choice but to submit to the will of God, trusting Him wholeheartedly. Again, the question arose, Why Lord? Why? I searched my heart, and the scripture that continuously repeated in my soul was Psalm 121: 1 and 2: "I will lift up mine eyes unto the hills, from whence cometh my help. My help cometh from the Lord, which made heaven and earth." I prayed over Tyler, anointed his ears with holy oil, and left it all to the Lord. My faith in the unknown had to take over. We scheduled the appointment and went to the audiologist at Blythedale Children's Hospital. She was phenomenal. Tyler went in during his scheduled time, no fussing or crying, and when the exam was complete, her report went like this:

"Mrs. Moore, I'm not sure what happened between the time you left the hospital and now. Maybe he had fluid in his ears, but his hearing is perfect, now."

I began to weep tears of joy and give praises to God immediately in that office. God is awesome and all powerful that He can do all things. To God be the glory for miracles.

As the months progressed, Tyler began to develop both mentally and physically. My home was very busy. The therapist would come in almost daily for occupational therapy, physical therapy, speech and special education service. In addition, I had to meet with the social worker who was assigned to his file. Medically, he was seeing his pediatrician, urologist, ear, nose and throat specialist, cardiologist, and ophthalmologist. There was always an appointment, and all of this had to be taken care of while I also maintained a full-time job. Based on the chart of progression as it relates to developmental stages, Tyler was lagging in some areas. One particular area was his muscle tone. During his Occupational Therapy and Physical Therapy sessions, one could see where Tyler was overcompensating other body parts to avoid using one particular body part. For example, Tyler's trunk area was weak, so to avoid using or strengthening this part of his body when crawling, he would "bear" walk to get around the house by walking on his hands and feet simultaneously. This was one of the items on the list during discharge that weakened my soul. I was told that there would be a great possibility that Tyler would not walk until he was at least three years old.

But God, God had a different plan. Tyler never crawled. He went from rolling around on the floor to pulling himself up to walking throughout the house on his hands and feet. He refused or just could not fix his body to bend his knees and crawl. Naturally or not, when other people see a child maneuvering throughout the house in such a form, it is seen in a different light and the questions begin to flow. Why does he do that? What's wrong with him? Why can't he crawl? Or people stared, pointed, and whispered. It did not make me, as the parent, feel welcomed when in public.

Again, I became overprotective and defensive. The anxiety of going to birthday parties were always a ten on a scale of one to ten, ten being the highest level of anxiety. Parents always asked insensitive questions about why he was not walking or saying certain words or constantly asking comparative questions. The persistent parents who wanted or insisted that I take him out of the stroller were overwhelming. If I decided to take him out of the stroller, it increased questions as to why Tyler maneuvered around the room the way he did. It always caused one of two reactions, snickers or whispers. The additional anxiety of birthday parties came with discovering that loud noises and overstimulation of colors and people was daunting and sometimes frightening. There were times Tyler would not enter a room or he would cover his ears and yell the word "no" numerous times. He would not move. He'd lock all his muscles or would flop down on the floor and relax all his muscles with dead weight. Then, there were other times when Tyler would stay and play with other children, but, not understanding his own strength or able to exhibit appropriate social play skills, he would push other children down really hard. Most times, I felt isolated because I had never experienced anything like this nor had I ever seen it. Occasionally, someone would ask, "How are you doing? Is there anything you need help with?"

In September 2009, Tyler was scheduled to have a circumcision. Due to his different ability, he could not have his circumcision done during birth. That crisp early fall morning at eight months old, jovial Tyler was prepped and ready for surgery. My husband and I were beyond nervous that he was going under anesthesia. We prayed, kissed him, and trusted that God had him and covered him. One hour later, the surgery was successful, and Tyler was in recovery. Within a few hours, he would be prepared for discharge. The doctor and nurse came in to explain the post-surgery care, then he was discharged. We made sure his medication was filled and provided the correct care when washing and cleaning his soiled pamper.

On the third day, early in the morning around 2:00 AM, Tyler let out a piercing scream that I had never heard before. I had just recently changed his pamper so I didn't check his pamper first. He was kicking and crying and screaming. I took his temperature to see if he had a fever, but it was normal. I tried giving him a bottle thinking maybe he was hungry, but he pushed it away. I then opened his pamper and began screaming myself because all I saw was a huge bubble of skin the size of a tennis ball where his penis should be. I immediately woke my husband up to help. He woke up in a frenzy and when he witnessed what was going on tears formed in his eyes. He told me to step aside because it may hurt Tyler more, but he had to relieve the pressure.

You see, the doctor did not remove enough foreskin from the penis area, and, as it was healing, the foreskin fused over the penis urethra area. This fusion did not leave an opening for any urination to release and it formed a huge bubble under the skin. My husband had to pull the foreskin back, breaking the skin to release the urine that was built up. The initial release was painful, but not as painful as the urine that was backed up under the skin. We then had to rush Tyler to the emergency room where they tried to insert a catheter through the urethra until the wound from the circumcision healed. We had to go through this process for several weeks because each time they thought it was healed, the foreskin would cover the penis and fuse over the urethra hole.

It was only by the grace of God that, on the last incident, I found the head urologist's home telephone number in an online directory in

New Jersey. I took a chance, prayed, and called the number listed. To my surprise, he actually picked up. I explained what we went through over the past month with each surgery and the numerous visits to the hospital. After hearing me out and overcoming the utter shock of my finding him at his home number, he advised us to meet him at the hospital at 8:00 a.m. the next morning so he could fix the issue.

However, fixing the issue would require Tyler having to endure another surgery and going under anesthesia again. It had been exactly eight weeks since the last surgery, but it felt like an eternity. But, it was a safe amount of time between surgeries for Tyler to undergo anesthesia without any possible complications. The surgery was successful, and I thanked God for His guidance, wisdom, and boldness to make that very necessary phone call. Through all of that, I thought once again, why me Lord? Is this what our life is going to be like? A life filled with tragedy, in hospitals, trauma filled, always with anxiety and feeling alone? Alone to the point that we think that no else is going through this? However, you placed me on assignment to receive children daily with a smile on my face as if there were no problems in my own life. I still went to work and received my students with LOVE. I had to sacrifice my own feelings and pity party to embrace the love of someone else's child. I really wanted God to let me have a do over and be a parent to a child who was not seen differently. Mentally, I had tapped out and left my husband to deal with all the issues while I went to work. I tapped out because I did not want to deal with the reality of life and having to manage and juggle schedules. I tapped out almost to the state of depression, thinking maybe if I did not go around people, I would not matter and just disappear. You know, out of sight, out of mind.

I was now a parent, though, and had to remind myself that I was neither allowed nor could I tap out as my parents tapped out on me. As a parent, I had to fight and advocate for my child with every fiber of my being and maintain a healthy mindset. As a parent, I was the only one who knew what was best for my son. As a parent, sometimes we are hesitant to go against the norm, but I encourage those parents to always go with your gut feeling, following what you think is right for your child. For the word of God tells us in Psalm 31:3 "For thou art my rock and my fortress; therefore, for thy name's sake lead me and guide me." As a parent, I had to believe that against all odds, Tyler would be different, but through his differences, HE IS WONDERFULLY MADE!

Due to Tyler's low muscle tone, there were areas of his body he needed to work out often, and, boy, did he resist and resent doing the exercises. We continued to push him and stretch him beyond his comfort. We did not baby his different ability or use it as an excuse or crutch to give up. We helped him work through difficult areas and he became resilient. It was not easy, and there were days I privately sobbed and cried the ugly cry.

One day while at the babysitter, Tyler decided he was going to take his first step. As exciting as that was, I have to tell you, as his mom, I felt guilty because I was not there to witness that incredible moment. I was taking a training class during my summer time off and wished I could have been home to be a part of this first and only time Tyler would take his first step. I had to hear about it over the phone. It was July 2010, Tyler realized he could stand up and balance himself, weeble wobble, put one foot in front of the other, and walk! I was excited and disappointed at the same time. Excited that he was walking and no longer "bear" walked, disappointed because I was not there. I was eager to leave training and get home to witness Tyler's new skill for myself. These were the steps in a new direction that he would take for the rest of his life as he began to defy the odds that were set by medical professionals. It has been history from that day forward. He got stronger, more coordinated to the point where he is so independent one would have never known he "bear walked." He began walking at eighteen months versus three years old. Faith in action, because Faith without works is dead. Tyler literally walked by faith.

Another different ability that Tyler struggled with was his speech. Due to the low muscle tone that most Trisomy 21 children have, communication through speaking can be difficult because speaking requires a great use of our muscles. Many Trisomy 21 children have what is called a protruding tongue or lazy tongue that naturally hangs outside the mouth in a resting position. Tyler's tongue does not do that. However, he does have some difficulty speaking clearly and articulating his thoughts so that the average person can understand him. As human beings, we know that communication is key to functioning successfully in society. Dr. Jonathan Shaw often said, "The lack of communication is the cancer to all relationships."

Therefore, early intervention was key, especially for Tyler in the area of speech. We began speech therapy at six months. The therapist would come in and read while also teaching sign language to Tyler.

We learned sign for his basic needs so we could communicate without his getting frustrated. These words included, but were not limited to, eat, milk, more, down, up, play, wet, juice, water, and ball. As he got older, the vocabulary list grew, and he began incorporating the use of words with sign language.

Then, one day we realized a pattern in his speech. Tyler would drop the first syllable to a word when he was verbally saying it.

So when Tyler wanted a snack, he said, "Mama udding."

I said, "Ugh, say that again Tyler. Mommy didn't understand."

"Udding".

Still not quite grasping this new word, I asked him to repeat it.

"Udding," Tyler said.

This went on for about five minutes. He was frustrated. I was frustrated. I was still trying to guess, calling out all kinds of toys. He finally asked me "up". So I took him out of the high chair, and he went over to the pantry where the snacks were. With an attitude, he grabbed the chocolate pudding cup and yelled "udding" at the top of his lungs. This incident made me feel helpless, dumb, and uneducated all rolled up in one. For the mere fact that I was not able to figure out what seemed so simple for a toddler as "pudding", I just could not get it without a visual prompt. This helped me understand the importance of slowing down my thinking process, how I analyzed a situation, to be inclusive of all and to listen to hear versus listening to respond. This helped me understand that silence is a response as well. When we are silent, we are able to see beyond the obvious. This incident helped me put life into perspective. Simplistic thinking can make life much easier. It can bring one to tears and bring joy at the same time. I was elated that Tyler was using and incorporating new vocabulary words while also silently chuckling about the verbal battle we just encountered, which almost brought me to tears. Psalm 126:5 reminds us that, "They that sow in tears shall reap in joy."

As a parent of a child with a different ability, there are moments you feel isolated, as if you are the only one going through a situation. Most times you may experience a particular situation with your child and at the moment you may be alone. But, rest assured, you are not the only one who has been in a helpless situation, or an embarrassing situation, or an emotional situation. There are other parents who are going through similar situations. It may not be identical to yours, but we can relate. The key is, recognize and accept that your child is different, that it is okay, and it is not your fault.

For me, I knew I had to connect to my spiritual Father daily because I was beating myself up, hiding behind being busy, unable to face the reality of having a child with a different ability, and my family was falling apart. But, God reminded me to seek Him first and His righteousness and all things would be added unto me. The scales from my eyes would be removed to see the blessing and beauty of God's love before my very eyes. To witness pure love, unconditional love in action. To embrace and be in the fullness of God's miracles. God chose me to be the mother of Tyler. He helped me love more, be more patient and understanding, fulfill my assignment, listen more and talk less, pray more, forgive more, be more kind, laugh more, live more abundantly, and always be reminded to give God the Glory for the great things He has done. For He is the Light.

Chapter 3 Reflection (Use space below to jot down thoughts)

1. How do you encourage yourself when going through difficult situations or just in general?

2. Write down the time you felt your faith was being tested the most. How did you get through it? If you had a chance to do anything different to get through the situation, what would you do?

3. Mental illness is a taboo topic in most communities, how can we help bring more awareness into the communities we serve?

4 A MOTHER'S LOVE

1 CORINTHIANS 13: 4-8

4 Love is patient, love is kind. It does not envy, it does not boast, it is not proud. **5** It does not dishonor others, it is not self-seeking, it is not easily angered, it keeps no record of wrongs. **6** Love does not delight in evil but rejoices with the truth. **7** It always protects, always trusts, always hopes, always perseveres. **8** Love never fails.

Love is patient, kind, always protects, always trusts, always hopes, always perseveres, and it never fails.

A Mother's Love is Patient. Having a child with a different ability has taught me to be patient in more ways than one. I used to have a one track mind regarding timeliness and not really an understanding spirit for those who were habitually late without hearing their story. Well, after having a child with a different ability who beats to his own drum, this mindset quickly changed. Having patience is defined as the ability to accept or tolerate delay. This was a lesson I had to get used to. Tyler entered preschool and kindergarten, and one of the prevailing issues was one particular behavior called "flopping". Flopping is defined as the means to fall or to hang loose. Well, someone with Trisomy 21 has the ability to relax all his muscles and it becomes dead weight when he flops. As mentioned previously, Tyler struggled with expressing himself. For example, if we were enjoying an activity and did not want to leave, most people verbally express displeasure with departure. Tyler, on the other hand, most times will not choose to use his words. Instead, he will flop by sitting down on the floor. Because of Tyler's size, he knows that, in most instances, if he flops, no one could get him up from that position without a real serious struggle and/or injury. Tyler knows that when he flops, he wins the battle. As his parents, we let anyone who will have immediate supervision over Tyler know what the possibilities are, especially during the times of transition, which have been Tyler's most often and frequent triggers. This behavior also manifests itself during any period of change for Tyler. The change can be with people, places, scenery, routines, expectations, speech volumes, voice tones, the word "no", and rules. We realized that anyone interacting with Tyler must be explicit, direct, and without any distractions or there was a great possibility, he would flop. The waiting period to change this behavior could be as long as hours or as immediate as a minute. I learned to be patient, build in sufficient time when planning any outings, and communicate if we will be late or not in attendance if need be.

Every day is different, and most times predictable. However, when it is not, we are reminded that Love is Patient.

A Mother's Love is Kind. To be kind is defined as having or showing a friendly, generous, and considerate nature. Tyler has a kind and loving spirit. For the most part, he is overly friendly. We have worked hard in teaching him boundaries with regards to being in other people's personal space. Due to the low muscle tone, Tyler had a natural tendency to want a hug, but with initial contact, he would crash into the other person's body. If it was his peer, he would knock them down. If it was an adult, he would not do so, but if caught off guard they would lose balance anyway. As a mother of a child with a different ability, every morning I would greet Tyler with "Big Hugs" giving him the hugs with extra pressure that he sought so when he was in school, he would not seek out this pressure from his peers and other adults.

In addition to the kind touches, kind words are important to

Tyler. Words are triggers that can cause a change in Tyler's behavior. This includes, but is not limited to, an adult's attitude toward Tyler. If he senses anger, he will shut down. He loves to be praised. To Tyler that is an expression of Love. If you deny a request, try to leave an activity without warning, or abruptly change something he is already engaged in, Tyler will shut down, and the effects will most likely result in flopping. This must be planned out explicitly without raising your voice or seeming annoyed, irritated, or upset. There cannot be an influx in your voice or he will shut down. I have found that if I need cooperation from him, what works best are kind words and words of praise. There is a balance, but we are always prepared for the behavior that comes along with it as well as to help him cope with working through the behavior.

Every day is different, and most times predictable. However, when it is not, we are reminded that Love is Kind.

A Mother's Love Always Protects. To protect is defined as to keep safe from harm or injury. As a mother of a child with a different ability, I found myself always in this heightened protection mode, especially because Tyler had no concept of danger as we know it. He has an overwhelming desire to be independent, but doesn't quite understand boundaries and danger (i.e. look both ways to cross the street or flopping wherever he is). While this behavior is understood in his school building, it is often misunderstood in other settings. There are stares, children pointing and laughing, or adults getting frustrated with his behavior.

One time, Tyler, his Pop-Pop, which is my father, and I took a trip to Grand Central Station on the Metro North train to give Tyler the experience of riding the train. Going into New York City was great. Tyler loved it. It was a new experience, a new feeling. On the express train, the conductor let him wear the conductor's hat. Grand Central station was the last and final stop. Everything seemed to be going well. But, when we got inside Tyler had a moment. Open space, stimulation on overload, too many people, different sounds, lights, etc. Tyler wanted to run, and mommy needed to keep him safe. Needless to say, the people of New York City were not the friendliest either. So, in order for Tyler to hear me, I had to raise my voice. Low and behold, Tyler flopped and wanted to go into shut down mode in the middle of Grand Central Station near the big clock. I was sweating. My dad had never seen this behavior, and he was aggravated and embarrassed. So now, I had to manage two behaviors.

Finally, we were able to get Tyler back on the next train home. Already knowing that his behavior was heightened, I begin to prepare his exit several stops away. One stop away from our final destination, Tyler began to shut down. The train pulled up to our final destination, and Tyler flopped as the doors opened. I had to drag him off the train onto the platform or endure a possible ride of two hours on an express train going north of our stop. I felt anxiety to the point where most parents retreat to the confines of their homes where it is safe and easy. At home, parents do not have to worry or be on high alert at all times like the park or during family gatherings or functions. Some parents do not find it comforting to hang out or have a playdate. I encourage parents to have more empathy when interacting with parents of children with different abilities, especially if a parent says, "I got it, thank you." Please respect that the parent really has the situation under control. Most times, adults want to solve the problem before asking the parent if it is okay to help. Also, most times parents and children with different abilities are not included, let alone, even invited to any special occasion events of their peers. Offer a helping hand to the parents of children with different abilities and try extending an invitation. It will put a smile on their face, and warm their heart. Do not stare and watch but ask and do. One's compassion and listening ear could make a difference. All it requires is a little time.

Every day is different, and most times predictable. However, when it is not, we are reminded that Love always protects.

A Mother's Love Always Trusts. Trust is to believe that someone is good and honest and will not harm you or that something is safe and reliable. As a mother of child with a different ability, you have to believe and trust that the adults that your child comes in contact with will do good, be honest, and will not harm your child, especially those children who are not able to articulate or communicate in a manner that all adults can understand them.

I had to learn to trust. My natural instinct is not to trust easily based on my past experiences. I am a natural observer of behaviors, and if one's behaviors do not sit well with me, I do not trust easily. In addition, if something is done to lose my trust, I forgive, but will always wonder what if? However, as a mother of a child with different ability, I had to let go of this willingness not to trust based on past experience because I was on a journey where needing others would be a part of my life.

There is a distinct difference between discernment and trust. Therefore, relationship building with Tyler is extremely important. If one does not connect with Tyler and build a relationship with him, one will not get any progress out of Tyler. As much as I must trust, Tyler has to trust even the more. In every aspect of Tyler's journey, I had to live by Proverbs 3:5-6, "Trust in the Lord with all thine heart; and lean not unto thine own understanding. In all thy ways acknowledge him, and he shall direct thy paths." I had to use my trust when picking those who worked with Tyler, whether it was a therapist, doctor, teacher, babysitter, or specialist. I had to trust the relationships that Tyler developed.

Every day is different, and most times predictable. However, when it is not, we are reminded that Love always Trusts.

A Mother's Love Always Hopes. Hope is defined as a feeling of expectation and desire for something good to happen. As a parent of a special needs child, we live on the feeling of hope. We are always hoping for the best. My daily discussion during the school week for Tyler was that he had consistent behavior of being on "Green" and being a first time listener. That is my daily hope and our goal.

We have to plan explicitly so that Tyler can stay on task, or he will immediately want to do something that is not part of the plan. Planning and having things laid out ahead of time was crucial. We used the following:

- First Then Board with stars as a reward
- Timer to indicate a change
- Give a countdown 15 minutes out (the longer the better)
- Give him a job as a leader (responsibility because he loves praises)
- Create a song or dance (he loves music and acting silly)
- Be consistent (too much change confuses him)
- Be mindful of the environment we are exposing him too.

Over stimulation will trigger him to behave differently and unfavorably (i.e. instruments, too much sound, too loud, too many people, too dark, too light, too many colors, too many choices, open room, open fields, jumping machines, microphones that are not being used, stages, costumes, characters, textures.)

As a parent of a child with different ability, I hope daily that he will overcome some of the triggers that make him different and make it challenging for him to sit normally in a setting. I hoped during his early years that he would overcome many obstacles, and he did. In

Tyler's time, he walked, talked, ate new foods, drank out of a cup, held and ate from a fork and spoon, went step over step up and down stairs, jumped and ran, climbed up monkey bars and a slide, potty-trained, learned his letters and numbers, wrote, read, performed in front of a large crowd, operated an iPad and computer, held conversation, and was able to get a haircut like a big boy. These may seem like small things to some, but these were my past hopes, and now are a part of Tyler's accomplishments list.

Every day is different, and most times predictable. However, when it is not, we are reminded that Love always Hopes.

A Mother's Love Always Perseveres and It Never Fails. This is the kind of love that continues in a course of action even in the face of difficulty. Love is truly an action word. It requires one to do something. It requires one to dig deep, to look beyond one's self and push forward no matter what. That is what a mother's love is like for a child with a different ability. There are times when you just want to cry or have cried out of frustration because you did not know what else to do. You feel like giving up because some days it is just seems incredibly hard to manage the behaviors, and there is no outlet for you. You still have to be mommy to everyone else, wife, co-worker, manager, friend, family member, and leader while balancing it all out. A mother's love is love in action and Dr. Seuss describes a mother's love best, "You know you are in love when you cannot fall asleep because reality is finally better than your dreams." Tyler, thank you for making my dreams a reality by choosing me as your mother.

Every day is different, and most times predictable. However, when it is not, we are reminded that Love always perseveres and it never fails.

Chapter 4 Reflection (Use space below to jot down thoughts)

1. There is an African Proverb that says, "It takes a village to raise a child." Have we embraced this value or disconnected from this? Why?

2. A mother's love has all the qualities of the Bible verses I Corinthians 13: 4-8: Patient, Kind, Protects, Trusts, Hopes, Perseveres, Never Fails, Does not envy, Does not boast, Not proud, Not self-seeking, Not easily angered, Keeps no records of wrongs, Does not delight in evil, but Rejoices with truth. What happens to a mother when some of these qualities are not reciprocated in a relationship or given back to her through her children? How does she continue to give out these qualities to her family?

3. As a mother/woman what do you do for yourself as an outlet? (daily/weekly/monthly)

5 HIS PROMISE WILL NEVER FAIL

GENESIS 17:16

"And I will bless her, and give thee a son also of her: yea, I will bless her, and she shall be a mother of nations; kings of people shall be of her."

We often hear throughout our lifetime never to question God, His will, and His way in our lives. I was reared to reverence God and not question the things that He did in our lives. At an early age I did not quite understand what that fully meant. However, when I was faced with trials and tribulations, I had to activate my faith and not my questions.

If I can be fully transparent and real with those who are reading, there were many times over the course of these past nine years of being Tyler's mother that I questioned God. From the very first phone call to the last Obstetrician-Gynecology appointment, I questioned God. I questioned God, asking why did you choose me to be Tyler's mom? Why did this happen to me? Why did this happen to us? Why did this happen to our child?

I remember so vividly trying to sort through all my emotions, fears, doubts, and confusion. I became increasingly anxious. I feared the unknown and what was to come. I had no idea what life would be like as a parent of a child with a different ability. I did not have a blueprint, and I felt like no one could help me dissect this new roadmap, let alone read it or direct me. This was like learning a new language. Between the huge amounts of paperwork for approval processes that were never a guarantee, to renewal paperwork, and always an appointment, I started to feel alone, as if no one else understood what I was going through.

For some reason, people around me did not openly discuss resources or feelings of raising a child with a different ability. Luckily, my profession afforded me an opportunity to learn, and I had no idea how much I would need it. I sat on an annual review meeting for the committee on special education as a summer assignment, so I had some knowledge of terms. Otherwise, I would have been like a deer in headlights with all the acronyms and lingo that were used during many meetings when discussing Tyler.

Then, one day, I sat in on a professional development training, and a colleague shared her story about being a parent and an administrator of a child with different abilities. This took place during the summer of 2011. My colleague read the poem, "A Trip to Holland" by Emily Perl Kingsley. She read the poem with such passion. Every word of the poem connected to every doubt and every fear that I had felt. "A Trip to Holland" expressed the very words that happened to me during my pregnancy from conception to delivery. It painted a picture of what we would have to deal with on our journey. The poem was a great way to express the very basic emotions that I went through. I still questioned God because, unlike the plane discussed in the poem, there were times it felt like the plane never landed, but re-routed to another location and then another, and another. When Tyler had to have his circumcision corrected, which required him to go back under anesthesia, it just felt as though I was going on another plane ride, another trip that I did not sign up for. Another destination that I may not be prepared for physically and emotionally. I feared that my child would not make it. I questioned

God again. I feared the what if. What if he didn't make it through? What if it was too early for him to have surgery again? What if the surgeon made a mistake again? What if the hospital made an error as they did in the past with someone else's child? God, what if?

Heavenly Father, thank you for Grace, Mercy, and Peace. Peace that surpasses all my understanding. Your love and grace are sufficient. I ask that you cover my child with your anointing and healing power. I ask that you touch every surgeon, doctor, nurse, specialist, attendant, utensil, instrument, and servant leaders who will be in Tyler's care. If you find it fitting in your will to allow him to live, let his personality and love be larger than life so that we will have no choice but to give you the praise, honor, and the glory. We will tell the world that you are the true and Living God and there are no gods before you. You are a miraculous God who will answer sincere prayers. Thank You, Lord, for listening and loving. For it is in the matchless name of Jesus the Christ I pray. Amen.

When you are rearing a child with different abilities you have to prepare yourself for a life filled with a lot of tulips and windmills, but also a lot of additional and very difficult obstacles. However, His promise never fails. You see, I prayed. I prayed that God would send me a son. He did just that, but He did it even better than I imagined. He blessed me with a son to allow me to teach and love in a different light. The bible states in Genesis 17:16 that "God blessed her twice, gave her a son, allowed her to mother nations and the kings of people shall be her."

God blessed me with Tyler because I was equipped for the task and chosen for the assignment. God found it necessary to bless me with Tyler because he pulls the best out of me as a human being, nurturer, advocate, educator, mother, disciple, servant leader, wife, better person, entrepreneur, and author.

Mornings have been challenging in our household. The most difficulty time of the day to manage is mornings. As mentioned in previous chapters, Tyler does not do well with change, so typically my husband has been in charge of morning duties. Due to my occupation, my schedule never permitted me to consistently assist with the morning routine. Our schedules normally were as follows: I worked days and my husband worked evening, allowing him to be in charge of morning duties. One particular morning, my husband needed to put something in his car and I got in the shower while Tyler was still sleeping (so we thought).

When my husband returned from the car, he came into the bathroom frantically questioning, "Is Tyler in there?"

I responded, "No. I thought you said he was asleep."

He responded, "He was when I left."

My husband then yells, "Tyler is not in the house Naima."

This is a mother's worst nightmare. I entered panic mode trying to find my glasses and something to put on my feet. Finally, when I get my bearings, I realized my husband had already left the house without me and I had no idea which way he went. My thoughts originally were to divide and conquer, but I didn't know which way to go. My heart felt like it was pounding in my esophagus. I was trying to contemplate whether or not to wait for the elevator that was coming up from the garage or take the stairs. At that point, I began to pray. God please protect my baby. Please keep him safe. Please put your angels of protections around him. Lord, lead me in the right direction to know which way to go, to take the stairs or wait on this elevator that may have Tyler on it. In the name of Jesus. Your Blood still works. Amen.

You see, where we live the main lobby leads out to an extremely busy street during morning rush hour. The busyness of the street includes cars, buses, trucks, taxies, and school buses. Tyler has no sense of danger and does not comprehend the difference between walking on the sidewalk and out in the busy traffic. My mind was racing and I did all that I could to block the what if's out. When the elevator doors opened, there stood Tyler with his pajamas. He had no shoes on his feet along with my anxiety filled, thankful, almost lifeless face husband.

Let us rewind back a little. When my husband went to his car and while I was in the shower, Tyler got up from his sleep and realized that his dad went out the door. He proceeded to follow daddy. However, daddy did not know. He left the house with his pajamas and no shoes on his feet by opening the front door. Tyler then closed the door behind him, walked down the hallway, and pushed the elevator to retrieve him from the floor he was on. Once on the elevator, he pushed the letter G to go to the lower garage where my car was parked. The elevator opened to the lower level, which looked like a boiler room area. Tyler pushed the crash bar on the door to exit the door to the garage area where automobiles move frequently in and out during this time for work. He went to my car, which the car doors happened to be open that morning, and climbed into the driver's side and began to play with the lights and horn as if he were driving. When my husband reached the garage, Tyler was in my driver seat honking the horn having a grand time, laughing and playing. The driver side door opened and Tyler's response was, "Look daddy, I'm driving."

But God! As Tyler's mom I knew from experience that God's promises never fail because God's spirit does not allow me to do things that are beyond my capacity. God has promised to never leave me or forsake me. So, as I struggle on each new route and journey, I seek God first. It may sound cliché to some, but it is that very thing that keeps me on course. It helps me not continue on the path of "Why Me", not to go down a deep, lonely path. I seek God to help me figure out those difficult moments when all I can do is cry. I seek God first to help me not to scream at the top of my lungs in frustration at Tyler or someone else. I seek God first to help me get to that peaceful place, when I need clarity and questions answered. There are many times where I just need to sit still. However, in those still quiet moments, you must know the difference between your own thoughts and God's voice. You must know the voice of God in the quiet time and only through your relationship with Him will you ever be able to know the difference. Only through seeking Him first, only through prayer, only through spending some time reading the Basic Instructions before Leaving Earth (Bible), will you ever know the true voice of God. In your prayers, ask for discernment, so that you know how to walk closely with Him in those times of trouble, frustration, confusion, hurt, pain disappointment, and anxiety. Ask for discernment to make the right decisions, discernment to have Faith and not lean on our own understanding, but in all that we do acknowledge God and He will direct our paths. For John 10:4 says, "My sheep know my voice and follow me wherever I Lead" all because HIS promises never fail.

Chapter 5 Reflection (Use Space below to jot down thoughts)

1. What does it mean to activate your faith and not question God?

2. Have you ever feared the unknown? If so, how did you overcome this fear? What steps did you take?

3. Write out or discuss with a partner your daily meditation time. Explain in detail, explicitly, what you do? Include time spent, resources used, people you speak to, social media, write out your prayers.

6 HIS NAME IS VICTORY

1 CORINTHIANS 15:54-57

54 So when this corruptible shall have put on incorruption, and this mortal shall have put on immortality, then shall be brought to pass the saying that is written, Death is swallowed up in victory. **55** O death, where is thy sting? O grave, where is thy victory?

56 The sting of death is sin; and the strength of sin is the law.

But thanks be to God, which giveth us the victory through our Lord Jesus Christ.

#HeisRockinganExtraChromosome #HisNameisVictory

Hashtag, He is Rocking an Extra Chromosome; Hashtag, His name is Victory is how I would tag all of Tyler's pictures on social media for the mere fact that I know the importance of controlling the narrative of what is said about Tyler. I understand the importance of words and how words create, orchestrate, and destroy. Words have power, both in the written and verbal form, so much so that there is a book that has been published in its ***5th edition The Princeton Review: Word Smart*** by Adam Robinson. The definition of Words is a sound or combination of sounds that has meaning and is spoken by a human being. This is the means in which we communicate. The very thing that can build you up and celebrate you is the same thing that can tear you down and humiliate you. Words are significant and important to the destiny of who, what, and how Tyler will be reared as a child with different abilities. As his mother, I do my best to ensure that the narration of Tyler's life is communicated by the words we choose as parents and not by what others or societal norms have said he would or should be. The doctors said one thing, but God had a different plan. It is my responsibility as his mother to report the "BUT God" moments. Therefore, the narrative that was tagged to his existence was and will be #HeisRockinganExtraChromosome #HisNameisVictory!

His name is victory is also tied to the symbol of a butterfly. The butterfly, to the naked eye, is beautiful and it comes in various shapes, sizes, colors, and regions of this world. The butterfly is significant to our family for several reasons. One reason is the butterfly represents the symbol for the National Down Syndrome Association. Second, the butterfly goes through several stages of life before it is transformed into the beautiful insect that God created. Lastly, the butterfly was my mentor's favorite insect.

Although she is no longer here on this earth to share her love with Tyler, she always said as long as there is a butterfly my love is here. I remember the day when I gave birth to Tyler and her reaction. She was not in the best of health, but she was excited and her words were inspiring and uplifting. As my mentor, she always spoke life into my dreams. She was overjoyed beyond belief, and I did not quite understand why she seemed more excited than I was until she actually spoke these words, "this is the best news you could have ever given me. My Tyler will forever carry the legacy of my birthday so that you will never forget me Nai." The butterfly, the love, the joy, the laughter, the comic relief, the personality, and every birthday reminds me that I am the heir of victory which then makes Tyler the sole heir of victory as well.

According to the United States National Library of Medicine, "individuals with Down Syndrome have an increased risk of developing several medical conditions. About 15 percent of people with Down syndrome have an underactive thyroid gland (hypothyroidism). The thyroid gland is a butterfly-shaped organ in the lower neck that produces hormones" (https://ghr.nlm.nih.gov/condition/down-syndrome). Butterflies are symbol of hope. "The blue and yellow of the Butterfly: blue is a color that spreads happiness among people, and the color yellow also evokes happiness and creates a feeling of energetic quality in the body and mind as well as an optimistic view. When the yellow is mixed with the blue, it shows a mix of dependability and perseverance with optimism and a bright future ahead for people with Down syndrome. World Down Syndrome Day is March 21st, and is a day that expresses a global voice to advocate for the rights, inclusion, and well-being of people with Down syndrome. The month of October is United States Down Syndrome Awareness Month." DownSyndromeAwareness - www.diabled-world.com/diability/awareness/down-syndrom-awareness.php

The Butterfly Life Cycle

All butterflies have a complete metamorphosis, which can be

stated as a complete change or a complete victory when they become the adult. There are four stages of life they must go through: egg, larva, pupa, and adult. Depending on the type of butterfly, it could take a life cycle of one month or up to one year to complete.

During the first stage, the egg, the butterfly starts life as a small round or oval dot. They are usually found on a leaf. To the naked eye, the caterpillar growing inside the egg is invisible. This is similar to the life cycle of a baby fetus growing inside his mother during pregnancy. The baby is fragile and to the naked eye you cannot see the fetus growing inside the mother. However, with technology, such as an ultrasound, one can see and hear the life cycle and process of the baby. I remember our very first doctors' visit so clearly. It was June 25th, 2008, the best 36th birthday gift I could have received. I could hear a strong heartbeat and see that clear like egg feature in the midst of contrast of black and white streaks on the monitor. The sound was victorious to our souls. Life was growing inside my body. In addition to the first visit, I can remember the day Tyler was born. I remembered when he cried and I was able to look at him and kiss him upon his arrival into this world. This was a reminder that God was in control of all things and He is Victorious.

The second stage of the butterfly's life is the Larva (Caterpillar). When the egg hatches into a caterpillar, the caterpillar stays on the leaf that it hatches on because that leaf becomes its source of nourishment. The caterpillar needs to make sure that it is on a leaf that it likes because it must eat continuously. As they eat, they grow and expand. The caterpillars grow by molting or shedding the outgrown skin. If one had to compare this stage to a human life, this stage would be similar to child rearing stages from birth to age eighteen. As parents, we are responsible for the caring and well-being of our children to ensure the safety and protection of our children with every fiber of our being. This stage is the most important time that I found it necessary to open my mouth and speak victory over Tyler's future and success. You see, I discovered that I could not feel sorry for him or myself once his different ability was confirmed. I had to kick in action the very words I read daily and truly believe in my heart and mind the words in the Bible were for me. I had to believe that faith without works is dead. I could not just read them, I had to do something with those words. God is waiting on us to do something. Healing, victory starts with my voice. What I speak about my son and the future of my son starts with me opening my mouth.

My mindset had to change and in doing so I had to be authentic with my testimony so that others could be set free.

This book was the start of my scar that needed healing. The very testimony that was birthed from my womb will hopefully be the breakthrough that will set someone else free or give another mother victory to say I can get through this obstacle because there is hope. For the Bible tells us that we are overcome by the blood of the lamb and the words of our testimony. So, when the doctors told me to abort Tyler, I said No, His Name is Victory. When the doctors told me Tyler would be deaf, I said No, His Name is Victory. When the discharge papers read that Tyler would have a heart condition, would not speak, would not walk until he was three years old, and would not be able to read, I said No, His Name is Victory. You see, I still believe in a True and Living God who performs miracles, signs, and wonders, and that the power of life and death lies within our tongues. What we speak matters! So, during this stage of Tyler's life, I will bless the Lord at all times and His praises shall continually be in my mouth. #Heisrockinganextrachromosome #HisNameisVictory

The third stage is the Pupa Stage, which is also called the Chrysalis stage. Once the caterpillar has grown to its capacity, they form into a pupa. This is where the change takes place. On the outside, it just looks like a hard shell sitting dormant. While on the inside, a metamorphosis is taking place, a transformation is occurring. A caterpillar is turning into a beautiful butterfly and preparing for the final stage. As I continue to advocate for Tyler, each day brings something new. There are times I still struggle, but through the struggle I celebrate. There are times I still cry, but through the tears Tyler wipes my eyes and tells me it will be all better with a knock, knock joke and we laugh. As he gets older, we begin to ensure that programs are in place for him. We continue to shape the narrative of what is said about Tyler's future. He is capable of greatness, but we have to paint that canvas of the beautiful butterfly that no one can imagine. Our job as parents is to ensure that Tyler lives in VICTORY.

The Fourth Stage is the Adult Butterfly. When the caterpillar is done forming inside the pupa, the butterfly will emerge. The wings will be folded against the body and then it will flap its wings to fly. It will fly off in pursuit to find a mate, reproduce, and begin the life process all over again. This fourth stage may play out differently for Tyler, just as it may play out differently for each individual as they evolve into adulthood. We don't know what the future may hold for any of us, but what we do know is that God has been Victorious for Tyler because Tyler is talking, formulating sentences, asking questions, telling knock-knock jokes, loves to read, recognizing sight words, knows his alphabet, numbers, colors, can write clearly, can spell his name and write it, understands math concepts, and can go to a restaurant and order from a menu. Is he at grade level? No. However, he is showing progress. Is he able to excel and become victorious? Absolutely. I know this because I serve a God who reminds me that, "Now unto him that is able to do exceeding abundantly above all that we ask or think, according to the power that worketh in us" Ephesians 3:20. #Heisrockinganextrachromosome and #HisNameisVictory!

Chapter 6 Reflection (Use space below to jot down thoughts)

1. What is your name and the meaning behind your name?

2. What is your favorite color and why?

3. If you had to be described as an animal or insect, what would it be and why?

7 PERFECT LOVE THROUGH IMPERFECTION

DEUTERONOMY 6:5

"And thou shalt love the Lord thy God with all thine heart, and with all thy soul, and with all thy might."

In the beginning of the book, I asked the question what do you do when you feel like you are doing all the right things, but you always feel different? What do you do when you are doing what is right, but not getting any results? ASK FOR HELP! What I have found through this journey of life, being a wife, a mother, a career woman, a minister, the one everyone comes to for help, the burden is heavy and most times I would feel guilty about not being able to do it all or feel guilty if I carved some time out in my busy schedule to do something solely for me. The best thing that I have discovered is that when I have asked for help, I have found perfect love through my imperfections. What I have found is that it takes a lot of strength to ask for help. Most times we allow our pride to hinder us from seeking assistance from others. Let me rephrase that. I allowed my pride to hinder me from asking for help. Once we let down our guards, we can see that we all have so much in common, and when we go through life changing experiences that can shake us to our very core, the wounds of the past will determine our willingness to let go and be free or retreat and be wounded.

However, it is only the Grace of God that can turn on the light. Only the Grace of God is the Perfect Love. It is only the Grace of God that can be the light of Faith. It is only the Grace of God that illuminates the light in our hearts to forgive. It is only the Grace of God to dig deep to find that inner strength to ask for help. It is only the Grace of God that allows us to ask for the strength to guide us in the right direction, to put us in connection with the right people, to be in the right place at the right time, to have favor over all that we do. The Grace of God gives us strength to ask another mother, "how are you doing or do you need anything?" For the word of the Lord says that, "The Joy of the Lord is my Strength." But, so many of us do not find the inner strength just to ask for help. So many of us suffer in silence not understanding that we have the power to reach our full potential and the very freedom we desire in the action of just opening our mouths. You see, the Grace of God is upon our lives when we open our mouths and tell our stories, for we all have a story to tell. The Grace of God is upon our lives when we give our testimonies. There is freedom in living in His Victory. When we tell the stories of how God made a way for us, it is liberating. It provides hope for someone else. It is uplifting. It gives the person listening to our stories confirmation of the possibility, confirmation of His victory.

God's Grace is the only testimony that has me here today. Statistically, I was supposed to be strung out on drugs, a teenage mother, a drop out, on welfare, living in public housing, a victim of abuse, continuing the cycle of generational curses and soul ties. But God. I could have used my past as an excuse. I could have allowed the circumstances of my past to dictate my future. I could have gotten stuck in the narration of my past story and allowed it to take root in my mind as current day reality, but I did not. For it was only by the Grace of God that my maternal grandmother saw it within her heart to stand in the gap and change the narrative forever. It is by God's Grace that the narrative of my life could have been different, but I used my past experiences to help push me through difficult moments in life. It is my past experiences that give me the drive and determination to always do better and excel. It was only through the Grace of God that I got through the bad times of my past experiences. What I found most and true is that through our imperfections and our lowest points God's love is manifested the most. God is made perfect through our imperfections. People can see our true and authentic testimonies when we are at our lowest, when we are broken, and when we are imperfect. This is the very thing that brings us into a better relationship with one another. This is what LOVE looks like, when we are Wonderfully Made and Teaching and Loving in a Different Light.

According to Webster's Dictionary, "a scar is a mark left on the skin or within body tissue where a wound, burn, or sore has not healed completely and fibrous connective tissues has developed." The very definition describes something that was once perfect but is now left with a visible imperfection that has not had time to heal. When I look back over my childhood, there were some scars that were left. The scars that I thought were healed were merely just oozing sores with bandages over them. As I was writing this book, I had to relive all the emotions, pains, disappointments, horror, trauma, bullying, ridicule, and inadequacies all over again. The feelings that I had learned to suppress, learned how to mask, learned how to avoid, and learned how to overcompensate through eating and shopping, all resurfaced.

One of my spiritual leaders said in our coaching session one day, "I will be here for you to help you, but you will have to do the heavy lifting." Those words hit me like a ton of bricks, literally, when I began writing. There were days when I wanted to just give up and say forget it because the emotional pain seemed so unbearable. I cried so much trying to write the first two chapters. I didn't think I could get through it. Then, the day came when I had to speak my truth out loud to my mother. You see, we have talked about and around the situation of our past on numerous occasions. My mother has always done most of the talking. She has written me letters, and she has spoken her truth. I always remember listening to my mother tell her story, listening to her get out her truth of what happened. As we were editing the chapters, my writing coach explained that I had to read the first chapter of the book to my mother prior to its being published because she could not read "my truth" the same time the entire world would read it.

When I called my mother, I was excited to tell her about the book project, but I had mixed emotions about reading the chapter to her. I explained that I would be reading the first chapter of the book to her over the phone, and I would need her approval to publish the truth along with her feedback. She agreed. As I read the chapter to my mother, I realized that this was the first time I was actually telling her how I felt about my childhood experience. As I read the chapter to her, I began to cry because I felt like that twelve year old girl again, re-living and expressing those suppressed feelings for the very first time. I cried as if someone snatched the band aid off that thirty-three year old wound. I cried the ugly cry as if I had been holding on to that scar for thirty-three years and it had finally healed. I cried because not only did it feel like freedom to me, but I also think it helped to free my mother from any guilt or shame she may have carried. When it was all done, my mother was full of pride and joy.

She said, "I am so proud of you! I cannot dispute anything you wrote. The truth is the truth. The good part is, I am glad I am not in that same place. God saved me."

I was always afraid that if I spoke my truth that it may open scars and wounds in my family that I was not capable of healing or fixing. For years, I did not want that burden or responsibility on my conscience. Unfortunately, as a result, I suffered from wounds and was hemorrhaging internally, all out of fear of speaking my truth. The scars from my childhood have left marks throughout my life that some may have seen on the surface. However, within my soul, it has only been through the Grace of God that has allowed me to heal completely through the perfect will of God. The scars of my past and current times have drawn me closer to the Master. My scars have allowed me to take a closer look at myself and to examine myself more. I have asked the difficult question, "What is it that I need to change in me?" I applied this question in every aspect of my life, as a wife, a mom, in my profession, as a person, a minister, a family member, a daughter, a sister, a friend, and a servant leader. How can I be a better person? How can God put me back on the potter's wheel? How can God mold me differently? Use me Lord, to thine will, for I am imperfectly, perfect in your sight.

When I look back over my life and I think things over, I cannot help but shout out Thank You Jesus for ALL you have done. For I know it is only by the Grace of God, that I am where I am today and writing this book, the same brown girl who struggled to read. So, I know it is only by the Grace of God that I love to read now, that my quest to conquer words is fearless. It is only through the Grace of God that I have multiple degrees. It is only by the Grace of God that Tyler chose me to be His mother, so we can conquer the world telling our story, letting everyone know that we are all made in the likeness and in the image of God. He makes no mistakes. God's answers are always yes and Amen. It is only by the Grace of God that Tyler is a living, walking, and talking testimony of the goodness of Jesus Christ. Tyler has only just begun for He is Wonderfully Made! As his one and only mother, I am Teaching and Loving him in a Different Light. This is a reminder that you can do all things through Christ who strengthens you! For we are all perfectly imperfect in the sight of God.

Chapter 7 Reflection (Use the space below to jot down thoughts)
1. Explain a time when you had to ask for help. Explain why you chose this particular person to help you.

2. Think about and describe a situation from your past that left an unhealed scar.

3. If you had an opportunity to go back in history and change something in your life, what would it be?

8 PARENT RESOURCES

Questions to ask OBGYN

1. How many prenatal visits will I need to schedule?

2. (If you are over thirty-five) do I have any special risks?

3. What tests or screenings are recommended and requires

4. During the first ten weeks, what is the noninvasive prenatal testing?

a. If you test positive or have high risk, your doctor may suggest amniocentesis. Ask questions!

5. If you are taking any medication, disclose to your doctor and ask about side effects during pregnancy. Are the medications I'm taking safe for pregnancy?

6. What labor and delivery methods do you and your practice recommend and provide?

7. Do you have a list or network of specialists you work with or recommend?

8. Can I call or email if I have more questions?

9. Will you be my delivering doctor? If not, will I get the opportunity

to meet the doctor that will be delivering my child?

Questions to ask the Perinatologist

1. Why was I referred to a Perinatologist?
2. How many visits will I need to schedule?
3. Will you be a part of the delivery of our child?
4. What screenings and tests are: a. recommended? b. required? And Why?
5. Are the medications I am taking safe for pregnancy?
6. What should I expect from each of my visits? At what point will my visits change?
7. Are my health conditions in good control?
8. Do I continue to see you post-pregnancy?
9. What do I need to do to stay healthy during and after pregnancy?

Questions to ask if child is in NICU

1. Why is my child being placed in the NICU (Neonatal Intensive Care Unit)
2. What are the visiting restrictions?

3. Can I hold my baby? Do you let parents hold skin to skin (kangaroo care)?
4. Do you have someone on staff at all times that I can talk to in to answer my questions?
5. Do you provide family care services/counseling?
6. Can you tell me some success stones of babies and families that were promoted from the NICU with similar diagnosis?
7. What is all the equipment in the room used for?

Questions to discuss with child's school and how to advocate

Before leaving the hospital, request for help from the local/county social worker. The first years of your child's life and his/her development are critical and crucial. IDEA are mandated services by federal law where states are required to provide early intervention services for all children who qualify. Services include, but are not limited to physical therapy, occupational therapy, speech and language theory, special services

Ages 0-5

1. What does early intervention look like for me and my family?
2. When should early intervention start?

3. How can early intervention benefit our family?

4. What are the various types of early intervention and how does each type help our family?

5. What happens after early intervention?

6. What is CPSE (Committee on Pre-School Special Education)?

Ages 5+

7. What is CSE (Committee on Special Education) in education?

8. When is a good time and how can we have a conversation about my child's progress?

9. What can I do at home to support our goals?

10. How do we measure progress? How often and when/how is this communicated?

11. What does support look like for my child?

12. What does the makeup of the class look like and is this the least restrictive placement available for my child?

13. What opportunities are available for parent training, transitional training, OPWDD process, ACCESS VR?

14. Who is the transitional coordinator and what role does

he/she have in educational planning for my child?

15. How can I gain access to a network list of Parent Advocates that are in my area?

Questions to ask Therapist

1. Why are we being referred to a therapist?

2. What is the recommended length of time that was approved for each therapist?

3. Who will provide support for my child during school hours?

4. How often is the support given to my child? What do you need from the pediatrician to begin services?

5. Is the support given at home, in the office, at school? If at school, is this a group setting, individual, or push-in model? Please specify with details.

6. How often do you support the classroom teacher? What does this look like for my child?

7. What can we do at home to support the goals of the therapist?

8. Is medication an option for therapy? What is the right of refusal? Do you provide alternative medication treatments?

9. Is family counseling available?

10. What special equipment/clothing/shoes are required to participate in therapy?

Top Ten Ways To Support Yourself

1. Find Time For Yourself! - Relax and find time to do something you enjoy or that puts a smile on your face.

2. Celebrate All Things - Everything that you do and accomplish, celebrate it! Your role as a parent of a child with a different ability can be taxing. Celebrate the little things.

3. Trust Your Instincts - You are your child's number one advocate, don't be afraid to speak for him/her. You know what will work best.

4. Make Time For Your Marriage - A marriage is hard work alone. Now add in a child with a different ability, that's even harder. Date each other like you just met for the first time.

5. Allow Grace to Manifest - Do not beat yourself up, we all make mistakes. Take a deep breath and exhale.

6. Accept Help - If someone extends their time to you, accept the help even if they do not do it your way.

7. Create a Wish List - Write down your wants and needs as a parent. Write down a name that can help you achieve that goal.

8. Organize Your Schedule - Keep a calendar of events appointments doctor visits, birthdays. Make sure it is visible stick to the schedule.

9. Keep showing up and tell Your Story - Stay in the present. Do not relive the pain of the past. However, tell your story and be vulnerable to the scary emotions. It is therapeutic and healing.

10. Energy and Money - Being a parent is exhausting, paperwork appointments research, meetings, communication books, setting goals, melt down, change in behavior and the list continues coupled with a full time job = energy zapping. Money requires extra care due to special attention, hours and needs.

Support Groups

1. Down Syndrome Association of Westchester

    85 Candlewood Road; Scarsdale, NY 10583; 914- 723-6568; ken@westchesterdsa.org

2. WARC Parent Assistance Committee on Down syndrome

26 Blackthorn Lane; White Plains, NY 10606; 914-654-0238; ebean37@hotmail.com

3. GiGi's Playhouse (Westchester)

720 Sawmill River Road; Ardsley; NY, 10502; 914-479-5566 westchester@gigiplyhouse.org

Tracy Smith, Program Director

4. Kids Health.org

5. National Down Syndrome Society (NDSS); www.ndss.org

6. Band of Angels

7. National Down Syndrome Congress (NDSC); www.ndsccenter.org

8. IncludeNYC - www.includenyc.org

9. NYS Partner in Policy Making - www.nyspip.org

10. Websites: www.downsed.org

www.ds-health.com

www.metlife.com

www.woodbinehouse.com

11. Westchester Institute for Human Development (WIHD) - Early Intervention:

Cedarwood Hall

Valhalla, NY 10595

Phone: 914-493-8150

Email: info@WIHD.org

Fun activities to do according to stages of development

Infant:

1. Mommy and I Time at Local Library

2. Pool Time

3. Park Time

4. Walks on Nature Trails

Toddler:

1. Mommy and I Time at Local Library

    2. Hands on Museums: Sensory Play is important

    3. Park Time

    4. Art and Music Therapy

    5. Pool Time

Pre-School:

1. Mommy and Me reading Time at Local Library

2. Gi-Gi's Playhouse

3. Parks and Recreation Special Needs Program

4. Hands on Museums

5. Park Time

6. Art/Music

7. Pool Time

Middle Childhood/Adolescents

1. Library programs for grade age students

2. Museums - Hands on

3. Art/Music - Play

4. Pool Time/Amusement Parks

5. Apple Picking

6. Restaurant Dining

7. Sports Programs

8. Special Olympics

9. WARC programming

10. OPWDD services

Chart of Progression

Gross Motor (physical) skills are those which require whole body movement and which involve the large (core stabilizing) muscles of the body to perform everyday functions, such as standing, walking, running, and sitting upright. It also includes eye-hand coordination skills such as ball skills (throwing, catching, and kicking).

Note: Each stage of development assumes that the preceding stages have been successfully achieved.

How to use this chart: Review the skills demonstrated by the child up to their current age. If you notice skills that have not been met *below* their current age contact Kid Sense Child Development on 1800 KIDSENSE (1800 543 736).

Age	Developmental milestones	Possible implications if milestones are not achieved
0 – 6 months	- Rolls over front to back and back to front - Sits with support and then independently	- Poor muscle development for locomotion - Delayed ability to play independently
6 – 12 months	- Crawls forwards on belly - Assumes a seated position unaided - Creeps on hands and knees - Transitions into different positions: sitting, all fours, lying on tummy - Pulls self to stand - Walks while holding	- Delayed sensory development due to decreased ability to explore the environment - Poor muscle development - Delayed play skills

	onto furniture • Takes 2-3 steps without support • Rolls a ball in imitation of an adult	
18 months	• Sits, crawls, walks • Still has wide gait but walking/running is less clumsy • Pushes against a ball (does not actually kick it)	• Delayed play skills • Difficulty interacting with the environment due to delayed ability to mobilize effectively • Poor muscle development
2 years	• Walks smoothly and turns corners • Begins running • Is able to pull or carry a toy while walking • Climbs onto/down from furniture without assistance • Walks up	• Poor muscle development for running and jumping • Delayed ability to play independently and interact with the environment • Decreased ability to interact socially

	and down steps with support • Picks up toys from the floor without falling overWalks smoothly and turns corners • Begins running • Is able to pull or carry a toy while walking • Climbs onto/down from furniture without assistance • Walks up and down steps with support • Picks up toys from the floor without falling over	
3 years	• Imitates standing on one foot • Imitates simple bilateral movements of limbs (e.g. arms up together) • Climbs jungle	• Decreased opportunities for social interaction • Poor development of body awareness and movement planning skills

	gym and ladders • Pedals a tricycle • Walks up/down stairs alternating feet • Jumps in place with two feet together • Able to walk on tip toes • Catches using body	• Difficulties using playground equipment • Difficulties or lack of confidence interacting with other children in active environments (e.g. play cafes, playgrounds)
4 years	• Stands on one foot for up to 5 seconds • Kicks a ball forwards • Throws a ball overarm • Catches a ball	• Lack of confidence in movement based activities • Difficulties using playground equipment • Difficulties or

	that has been bounced • Runs around obstacles • Able to walk on a line • Able to hop on one foot • Jumps over an object and lands with both feet together	lack of confidence interacting with other children in active environments (e.g. play cafes, playgrounds)
5 years	• Able to walk upstairs while holding an object • Walks backward toe-heel • Jumps forward 10 times without falling • Skips forwards	• May result in poor self-esteem when comparing self to peers • Lack of confidence in movement based activities • Difficulties participating in sporting

	after demonstration • Hangs from a bar for at least 5 seconds • Steps forward with leg on same side as throwing arm when throwing a ball • Catches a small ball using hands only	activities • Difficulties playing with moving toys such as bikes and scooters
6 years	• Runs lightly on toes • Able to walk on a balance beam • Able to skip using a skipping rope • Can cover 2 meters when hopping • Demonstrates	• Difficulty participating in sporting activities • May result in poor self-esteem when comparing self to peers • Lack of confidence in movement based activities

| | mature throwing and catching patterns | |
| | • Mature (refined) jumping skills | |

This chart was designed to serve as a functional *screening* of developmental skills per age group. It does *not* constitute an assessment nor reflect strictly standardized research.

The information in this chart was compiled over many years from a variety of sources. This information was then further shaped by years of clinical practice as well as therapeutic consultation with child care, pre-school and school teachers in South Australia about the developmental skills necessary for children to meet the demands of these educational environments. In more recent years, it has been further modified by the need for children and their teachers to meet the functional *Australian Curriculum, Assessment and Reporting Authority (ACARA)* requirements that are not always congruent with standardized research.

9 TEACHERS, FRIENDS, AND FAMILY RESOURCES

Advice for educators

1. Always set high standards for our children with a different ability. Do not water down the curriculum. You will be surprised how engaged that child will be in your class.
2. When speaking to parents, always find a way to say something positive about the child first.
3. Be caring, supportive and respectful toward parents.
4. Provide an open line of communication with your parents.
5. Avoid gossip and using labels to describe a student.
6. Always be willing to offer resources and information to

parents.

7. Choose your words carefully because every word matters and it can make or break their spirits

8. Be willing to seek assistance from others in the profession. Shadow a veteran, effective or highly effective teacher.

9. Seek out professional development opportunities to enhance your craft.

10. Be willing to take risks.

Advice for Family and Friends

1. Choose your words wisely. Understand what language you are speaking.

2. Ask clarifying questions when you don't understand.

3. Talk about your child and not about the disability.

4. Always find ways to talk about the strengths and abilities of your family member.

5. Teach all those who come in contact with you the appropriate words to use when talking about a child with different abilities.

6. Be caring, supportive and friendly to your family member in

need.

7. Encourage family members to ask questions and express their emotions.

8. Remind family members that they are not alone. They are not the first and will not be the lack.

Wonderfully Made By Fatima Scipio

You are beautifully and wonderfully made

When God had you in mind,

the foundation of your destiny was laid

From the top of your head, to the soles of your feet

You were beautifully and wonderfully made just for me

The apple of my eye, a light that shines bright

Completely blessed beyond measure to have you in my life

You help me to grow and know unconditional love

Only this kind of love could come from the creator of love

You are beautifully and wonderfully made

No weapon formed against you will ever prosper

Because the price was already paid.

I speak love and life over you my child

You were born to win, born to succeed

Born to be different and here is why

Because God said you are beautifully and wonderfully made.

ABOUT THE AUTHOR

A native of Yonkers and White Plains, NY, Naima attended Yonkers and White Plains Public Schools. She graduated White Plains High School, class of 1990. Naima attended North Carolina Central University in Durham, NC and graduated Cum Laude with a Bachelors of Business Administration in Finance, class of 1994. Naima began her first full time job at The Bank of New York where she worked as an assistant to the Vice President of Municipal Banking. Naima decided to obtain her Masters of Business

Administration (MBA) in Finance and Human Resource Management. In May of 1999, she graduated Cum Laude from Pace University, Lubin School of Business with a MBA. In October of 1997, Naima began her career at Diversified Investment Advisors where she was an Assistant Manager of the Call Center, a Financial Assistant, and a Manager of Finance & Human Resources of the Information Technology department.

In her spare time Naima has always been involved with helping children in the community, as a Youth Advisor, actively involved in Alpha Kappa Alpha Sorority, Inc. youth groups and currently the Youth Minister at Calvary Baptist Church in White Plains, NY. She has such a love and passion for children that she could not ignore her natural ability and calling to teach any longer. Naima took the step and decided to pursue her dream of becoming a teacher. In September of 2003, Naima was employed as a middle school teacher at Commerce Middle School in Yonkers, NY. In September of 2004, Naima was employed by White Plains Public Schools as a Business Educator at White Plains High School. At WPHS, she taught, 21st Century Computers, Marketing, Sports and Entertainment Marketing, Accounting, Finance and Business Management. While teaching and becoming involved in the school community, Naima enrolled in the SUNY New Paltz, Education Administration program and graduated in May of 2007. To further her commitment to life-long learning and her calling, in October of 2017, Naima completed the Institute of Youth Ministry Certificate Program at Princeton University Theological Seminary. In November of 2010, Naima was employed by Peekskill City School District as an Administrator and Extended Day

Coordinator at Peekskill Middle School and in July of 2016 moved with the class of 2020 to Peekskill High School as the Assistant Principal where she currently serves in this capacity. In addition to her busy work life, Naima is most proud of being an awesome wife to her husband Steven Moore for 11 years and a super awesome mom to their son Tyler who is 9 years old. Naima is a woman of God and truly believes that God placed her at Peekskill for such a time as this. She loves her students and staff members as family and always expects excellence from both. She lives by the motto: "To whom much is given, much is required" and being a "Servant Leader". Dr. Martin Luther King, Jr. said, "Not everybody can be famous. But everybody can be great, because greatness is determined by service. You don't have to have a college degree to serve. You don't have to make your subject and verb agree to serve...You only need a heart full of grace and a soul generated by love."